Faith in War the Soldiers Bible

Faith in War the Soldiers Bible

Zac Miller

Copyright © 2020 by Zac Miller.

Library of Congress Control Number:		2020905355
ISBN:	Hardcover	978-1-7960-9505-0
	Softcover	978-1-7960-9506-7
	eBook	978-1-7960-9513-5

All rights reserved. No part of this book may be reproduced or transmitted in any form or by any means, electronic or mechanical, including photocopying, recording, or by any information storage and retrieval system, without permission in writing from the copyright owner.

The views expressed in this work are solely those of the author and do not necessarily reflect the views of the publisher, and the publisher hereby disclaims any responsibility for them.

Any people depicted in stock imagery provided by Getty Images are models, and such images are being used for illustrative purposes only.
Certain stock imagery © Getty Images.

Print information available on the last page.

Rev. date: 03/23/2020

To order additional copies of this book, contact:
Xlibris
1-888-795-4274
www.Xlibris.com
Orders@Xlibris.com
809494

CONTENTS

SGT Jesse Maple, Vietnam 1
SGT Bill Maple, Vietnam 15
SGT Roger Hill, Vietnam 23
SGT Cliff McPeak, Iraq 39
SPC Zac Miller, Iraq 47
SGT Zac Miller, Kuwait 65
SGT Zac Allen, Iraq 79
CW2 Zac Miller, Kuwait, Iraq, and Syria 85
SGT Will Allen, Afghanistan 99

In Conclusion 103
About the Author 105

SGT Jesse Maple, Vietnam
April 1967–April 1968

In 1966, at the age of nineteen, Jesse was drafted by the United States Army. He was from a family of eight children, six boys and two girls. Nathan, Jesse's oldest brother, was the first drafted during the Korean War. Dean was the next to get drafted between Korea and Vietnam but, due to his medical class, was not taken for military service. Bernard was the next brother to be drafted and served his time in the army in the early 1960s, mostly in Okinawa, Japan, which was rare for a soldier in the army as marines were normally in this area. Sam was drafted next but was turned down for service due to his medical class as well. Jesse was next to get drafted in 1966. He stayed in until 1968 for his active service then inactive service until 1972. He then decided to join the Army National Guard in 1975, which he did at the time for the extra pay it would provide. Jesse eventually ended up retiring with twenty-five years in service. Jesse's brother Bill was the last to be drafted in 1967. Bill went to Germany with the army and then to Vietnam. Bill would also join the Army National Guard in 1990 because there was talk of Jesse's guard unit becoming mobilized for Desert Storm and he didn't want his brother to go without him. All six of the Maple boys were drafted.

Jesse would go to Fort Hayes, which was located in Columbus, Ohio, and was an induction center at the time. This was where he was given his pocket Bible by a group of Gideons. He put it in the breast pocket of his uniform, and that was where it would stay for the next two years. Jesse, at the time, was known for being a bit of a hell-raiser and a drinker. But he always believed in God, did the right thing, and helped those in need. From Fort Hayes, Jesse would soon head out to Fort Benning, Georgia for basic training and then onto Fort Polk, Louisiana for infantry training since he was an 11 Bravo (11B). After his infantry training, he was given a two-week leave. As soon as Jesse's leave was over, he boarded a plane and headed to Vietnam.

Jesse landed in Saigon, Vietnam, and was transported to the ninetieth replacement center, where he would stay for fifteen days waiting to be assigned a unit. You would be assigned to whichever unit had received the most casualties at that time, which, in Jesse's case, was the 196th Brigade (light infantry). He would be in the Fourth Battalion (BN), Thirty-First Infantry (IN), Delta Company (D Co), which, in mid-April 1966, had their headquarters in Chu Lai, known as the Chargers Academy, home of the 196th Infantry. D Co was located just off the coast of Chu Lai on a peninsula. The entire area was infested with Vietcong (VC). D Co would be splitting the area of operation with a small portion of the Third Marines. The marines were in charge of security for a docking area for a ferry that was responsible for bringing in supplies to the peninsula—mostly vehicles, food, and other essentials.

D Company's mission was to keep the roadways clear by doing daily minesweeping. The infantry teams would be spread out and would flank the sides of the roadway looking for any booby traps or VC ambushes. Jesse said, t this time, our biggest dangers were the booby traps and almost daily sniper fire from the VC that would never stand and fight always, a shot here or there, and then they would try to slip away undetected." However, D Co had adapted tactics of their own. They observed that the VC were very loyal people and would never leave a body. They would always return to collect their fallen comrades; it might be later that night or even a day or two, but they would be back. So that was when Jesse's section would set an ambush and wait sometimes a few hours right after nightfall; other times, they would have to lay in the jungle for two days waiting for them to return. It almost always paid off, and Jesse's section would be able to kill a few more of them.

Jesse said that the most effective weapons the VC had in their arsenal were mortars and rockets to use against them on that peninsula. D Co, being a light infantry company, had rifle teams made up of riflemen, grenadiers, and machine gunners. So the biggest weapons they had were the M60 machine gun and the M79 grenade launcher. If they needed indirect fire, they would have to call for fire from artillery stationed at Chu Lai, as all the mortars and larger-caliber machine guns were in the weapons company of the battalion elsewhere in Vietnam.

At this time, Jesse was the machine gunner; he carried the M60, which was the heaviest machine gun a light infantry company had. It fired a 7.62×51mm NATO round. The M60 weighed in at 23 lb, which helped earn the M60 the nickname Pig, mostly because of its bulkiness, not to mention the ammo you would have to carry for it. The M60 fired 7.62 linked (belted ammo). Jesse was only 5 feet, 6 inches and weighed 130 lb, so this was a substantial load he was carrying daily along with his ruck (a large backpack with frame). In his ruck, Jesse would have all the essentials he would need for survival in the bush for at least two days without resupply. Because of Jesse's size, he was the company's designated tunnel rat (a tunnel rat was usually a small-statured infantryman who would go into mostly Vietcong-controlled tunnels on search-and-destroy missions).

It is estimated that the VC had around 250 km of underground tunnels that they used during the Vietnam War. When Jesse would go into the tunnels, he would trade in his M60 for an M1911 .45-caliber pistol that held eight rounds and a flashlight. He cleared probably twenty-five tunnels during his time in Vietnam. In all the tunnels, he only ever came across two North Vietnamese Army (NVA) regulars, and they were both taken prisoner one at a time later on in his tour in Northern Vietnam. Luckily, they were both unarmed when he came upon them in the tunnels, and he was able to take them in as prisoners. The tunnels would then be blown up. Jesse recalled one incident when he cleared a tunnel and said he found a large room; it was where he surprised the one NVA regular and took him prisoner.

The room was ten-by-ten feet and looked as if it was being used as some sort of command station. This room was huge considering that the tunnels were usually only shoulder width, and a lot of times, you were not even able to stand up in them—you would only be able to crawl. Upon exiting the tunnel and reporting his findings to his commander, Captain Mellon, it was decided they were going to blow up the tunnel using a shaped charge. The shaped charge was flown into them on a helicopter and weighed 80 lb. It was all ready to go; all Jesse had to do was place it and hook up the detonating cord. Jesse was left with a radio and two other men to accomplish this task as the rest of the company spread out at a safe distance and set up a 360. After placing the shaped charge in the room in the tunnel, Jesse ran 150 ft of detonating cord out of the tunnel. The three men took up a position behind a large tree to blow it. It was at this moment Jesse realized he didn't have his clacker in his ruck. This was the device that you hook your detonating cord to so you can get a spark to set off your claymore mines or, in this case, the shaped charge that was in the tunnel.

Jesse began to panic; the other two frantically looked in their packs, but none of them had a damn clacker. Finally, one of the guys with Jesse came up with an ingenious plan. He told Jesse to just take the cable off the radio, hook one wire to the ground, and then just probe the other wire on all the pins until he found the hot one; and it would go off. Sure enough, *boom!* It worked! He said it seemed like the jungle was raining dirt, rocks, tree limbs, and all kinds of other debris on them for what seemed like an eternity. In reality, it probably only lasted for thirty seconds or so. Eighty pounds of C-4 definitely did the trick.

After Jesse was in country for about three months, he was promoted to corporal, which also meant he was now a team leader and would have to give up his M60 for an M16. Around this same time, General Wes Moreland was the theater commander, and he decided to move Jesse's unit to Tam Ky, which, at that time, was as far north as any regular army unit had been. This was when all the real brutal fighting started. They were fighting NVAs now, and for the most part, they would not run; they were very well equipped and would stand and fight. This was not at all like the VC Delta Co was used to fighting down south, who would harass and then retreat once contact was made and resistance was put up. Once Jesse's battalion got up north, they never had a base camp again. Fourth Battalion, Thirty-First Infantry, Delta Company became what was known as a roving battalion. This meant they slept under the stars every night and had no luxuries like showers or chow halls. Even through the monsoons, they stayed in the bush, never going into a base camp. They were on constant seek-and-destroy missions.

The worst battle Jesse was in was at the Que Son Valley, Hill 63. The valley sits forty kilometers southwest of Da Nang with Hill 63 sitting in the center of it. It was November 23, the day before Thanksgiving 1967. The plan was for the infantry companies to lead the fight backed up by the Seventeenth Cavalry and their tracked APCs (armored personnel carriers) with heavy machine guns mounted. D Co would have the job of securing the right flank of Hill 63. November is the beginning of the northeast monsoon season in that part of Vietnam. That morning reflected that with temperature in the low 60⁰s and low-hanging, seemingly unending fog and rain. After a C ration breakfast, the men strapped up their bulging rucksacks and started their cautious advance to Hill 63.

They started walking just as the first rays of daylight started to show at 0600 hours. Just as they reached the bottom of the valley and were nearing the base of Hill 63, Jesse heard a single crack of a rifle. Jesse said, "I thought some dumbass in one of the other sections had their finger on the trigger and had a negligent discharge." No more did he get that thought out when he heard someone yelling, "Polar Bear!" That was code for medic; someone had been shot. Then almost immediately to Jesse's left, a machine gun opened up, killing one of the guys from Jesse's platoon. Jesse dropped to the ground and took cover. He could see the machine gun firing down to his left. The enemy was dug in, and there was a thicket of bamboo between him and the bunker. He was scared as hell but knew it was up to him to silence that machine gun. Jesse pulled off his ruck and made a break for a knee-high rock halfway down the hill between him and the machine gun, only carrying his M16 at this time.

Just as he was nearing the rock, he started taking fire; and as he dove for cover behind the rock, a spray of bullets impacted it. He made it; he was behind that rock but was temporarily blinded. When the bullets hit the rock, they had kicked up sand and dust that went in Jesse's eyes. He wiped them, and while blinking, he was simultaneously reaching for his grenades. He soon realized they were attached to his ruck that he had shed off some fifty yards up the hill. Now pinned down by enemy fire, he had one choice; he yelled up to Bobby Shrum and told him to throw them down to him. He did, and it worked. Jesse now had three grenades. He quickly threw the first grenade at the machine gun bunker, which was about twenty-five meters away. It hit the bamboo thicket and bounced off to the side and went off. Jesse threw the second one just to have the same thing happen. Finally, on the third and last attempt, it made it and blew up, and the machine fell silent.

Jesse leaped up and ran to the bunker. The two NVA soldiers in the hole were still moving around, so he dispatched them quickly with a burst from his M16. At that moment, he looked to his right and saw an NVA soldier in full web gear and helmet with an AK-47 slung at the low ready. Jesse didn't shoot him because he thought he was one of the interpreters they had with them in their platoon. The NVA soldier turned and ran over a mound just as a .50-caliber machine gun started laying down heavy fire on the bunker Jesse was standing in. It was the Seventeenth Cavalry with their APCs. Jesse had no choice but to lie as flat as he could on the floor of the bunker, pushing the bodies of the dead NVA soldiers over so he could get as low as possible. The .50-caliber machine gun was ripping the bunker apart, blowing huge holes through the earthen walls. Taking that machine gun position was how Jesse earned his Bronze Star with the "V" device. A "V" device on a medal denotes valor and can only be earned in combat.

At this point, the battle for Hill 63 was in full swing. The dug-in NVAs were putting up a stiff resistance. Delta Company paid a large price during that encounter with the dug-in machine gunners; it cost them four KIAs (killed in action) and eleven wounded soldiers, five of whom were seriously wounded and required medevac choppers. The Seventeenth Cavalry had also taken one KIA, and several others were wounded as one of their APCs was blown up when the NVA shot it with a 57mm recoilless rifle. This was all by 0900 hours. The battle would rage on for a total of ten hours of intense fighting.

Later in the day, during the battle for Hill 63, Jesse was in charge of taking out a spider hole (a spider hole is a hole dug out usually with a cover that the NVA and VC would use to engage enemy from). They knew there was a single NVA soldier in it. Jesse decided to cook off a grenade and then throw it in as was common practice at the time. Jesse said, "If you didn't cook it off a lot of times, the gooks would just throw it back out at you." Jesse threw the grenade as hard as he could, but it hit a flap of woven banana leaves at the entrance and bounced back. Luckily, Jesse and his team were all behind cover and were not hurt. "The NVA soldier hiding in the very back of the hole threw a long-handle stick grenade back at us," Jesse said. It hit a tree that his lieutenant was directly behind and went off. This grenade blew shrapnel through the whole team. Jesse took a few pieces of shrapnel from that grenade to his left knee that he still carries with him today. He would be awarded his Purple Heart for that. Jesse cooked off another grenade, this time finding the entrance and killing the NVA soldier inside.

Later that night, after the fighting subsided, Jesse got his knee better tended to by the medic, who did a great job earlier and was able to get him patched up good enough that he was able to stay in the fight. Jesse could have bowed out of the fight right then with the shrapnel in his knee and gotten evacuated out off the frontline, but that wasn't Jesse. He had men under him who relied on him. Also, he couldn't let the men to his left and right down. The One Hundred Ninety-Sixth needed him more than ever at that moment.

As the unit sat there and treated the wounded and tried to get some food (C rations), the chaplain made his rounds, talking to all the troops. When Jesse saw him coming, he reached in his rucksack and grabbed a can of peaches that he intended to offer to Bernard Christy, the Catholic chaplain; but when he pulled it out, it was dripping everywhere and had a bullet hole through it. Then he pulled out his poncho liner and other gear, and they were just shredded. They were rolled up, so a couple of bullets probably did it, but it looked really bad.

When the chaplain saw this, he told Jesse, "The Lord was with you today." Jesse already knew this, but that was when reality really set in. That was why he carried his Bible and will continue to carry it with him. Jesse wasn't even Catholic; he was Methodist. But he said once the fighting started, the men never saw the Methodist chaplain as he didn't want any part of the danger of war. The next morning, Jesse prayed to the Lord that he would just take a round in the shoulder; that way, he would have to leave that hell. Soon the battle ended, and Hill 63 was clear. The unit Mermited their Thanksgiving Day dinner chow out to them. It had been held for them from the day before. Jesse said, "It tasted good but was spoiled apparently, as everyone got sicker than hell from it."

The result of the 196th's battle with the Second NVA Division for Hill 63 was, 128 enemy NVAs lay dead and seven Americans were KIA with another eighty-four Americans wounded. Hill 63 was declared a victory.

* * *

Over Christmas, things started looking up for Jesse; he was given R & R in Australia. He got there and drank some the first three days, then he started feeling sick, running a fever toward the end of his leave for the last three days. When he arrived back in Vietnam, he was taken to the navy corpsman in Da Nang. Jesse was coming in and out of consciousness and had an extremely high fever that lasted for twenty-two days. It ended up being malaria, but once again, Jesse had the Lord looking over him as he would make a full recovery.

After that bout with malaria, Jesse returned back to his unit and was promoted to E-5 sergeant and squad leader. His guys told him he had a new guy who was from Coshocton, Ohio, the neighboring town of West Lafayette, which was Jesse's hometown. They are a mere seven miles apart in the same county of Coshocton. The new private's name was Bill McCullough. Since they had so much in common, he was put in Jesse's squad.

The Tet Offensive was starting, and it wasn't long until the 196th was in heavy fighting again. Jesse recalled that D Co was in an intense firefight and pinned down pretty good when Captain Mellon was calling for fire (artillery) on the radio. At that moment, when he had his hand mic up to his ear, he was shot; he ended up surviving but had to be medevaced out and would not return to the unit. That day was a sad day for Jesse and D Co, as Captain

Mellon was a great commander. The guys looked up to him and his style of leadership.

Jesse's platoon got a call on the radio one day, toward the end of his tour, from a surveillance plane flying overhead that there were two NVA soldiers out in a clearing directly in front of them headed to the tree line. The job of Jesse's platoon was to go into the woods and kill them. This was the infantry's mission in Vietnam, a constant seek-and-destroy mission. As soon as they made it to the tree line, they realized that there was a large creek just inside it. They had to search the creek banks for them. One was spotted, and most of the squad fired into the water where he was hiding across the creek and under the water, breathing through a reed.

Someone had to retrieve the body. Everyone hesitated, so Jesse volunteered. He didn't feel like making one of his squad members do this task, as he knew the dangers it presented. This creek was deep, and Jesse was scared as hell, more of drowning than of the NVA soldier that was still unaccounted for. When Jesse got to the NVA soldier's body, he realized he was still alive. Jesse grabbed him firmly and waded back through the shoulder-deep water. When they got the NVA soldier up on the bank, it was clear he wasn't going to make it. He was hit a few times in the body and once in the head. Jesse said they tried to question him, but he wasn't making any sense due to shock. Before their officer got over to them, another member of the squad broke down and emptied his M16 on the NVA soldier. The other NVA soldier in the creek was never found.

Soon it was April 1968, and Jesse's tour was over. He returned home with his Bible still in the left breast pocket of his uniform.

He credits it with bringing him home in one piece. He would keep the Bible put up at his house and give it to the ones he loved when they would ship off to wars in the future. He did this in hopes that the Lord would watch over them as well on their journeys into harm's way.

Jesse earned quite a few awards over his twenty-five-year career in the military, the most notable being the Bronze Star medal with the "V" device. The "V" device means valor; it can only be earned in combat. Jesse earned this award during the battle at Hill 63 when he single-handedly took out that machine gun bunker. He also earned a Purple Heart medal for when he took shrapnel from a grenade in his left knee. He received a Combat Infantryman Badge—this badge is only awarded to infantry army MOS (military occupational specialty) of Eleven Infantry series or Eighteen Special Forces series for active ground combat with the enemy. He also received a Vietnam Service Medal with three bronze service stars, a Republic of Vietnam Campaign Medal with the "1960–" device, and a National Defense Service Medal. Humanitarian Service Medal—Jesse earned this medal while in the Ohio Army National Guard for performing humanitarian duties during the blizzard of 1978 in Ohio. His Bible was with him on this duty as well. He was also awarded the Armed Forces Reserve Medal with numeral 2, the Army Reserve Component Achievement Medal, the Army Service Ribbon, the Overseas Service Ribbon, and the Army Reserve Components Overseas Training Ribbon with numeral 3.

Jesse in his dress uniform

SGT Bill Maple, Vietnam

January 1968–August 1969

In 1967, Bill was given the option to either go to the army or go to jail by Judge Hickman. So, not wanting to go to jail, Bill went with a longtime friend and neighbor, Roger Hill, to Fort Hayes in Columbus, Ohio. They had the idea after talking to a local recruiter that they would join on the buddy plan. Unfortunately, not long after they got to Fort Hayes, they figured out that wouldn't be the case since Roger was turned down because of his criminal record. Bill went ahead and joined on what was known as the volunteer draft. So during in processing, the army took Bill and sent Roger home. However, just two weeks later, Roger would end up getting drafted anyway.

Bill was sent to Fort Jackson, South Carolina, for his basic training, then to Fort Bliss, Texas, to learn about and train on Nike Hercules nuclear missile systems as a crewman. His first duty station would be in Wertheim, Germany. In December 1968, Bill would come home on a two-week leave before he would have to report to Fort Lewis, Washington. That is where you would go to ship out for Vietnam at the time. While home on that two-week leave, Bill's brother Jesse was also home on leave from Fort Campbell, Kentucky. Jesse would give him the Bible that he carried in his left breast pocket while he was in Vietnam. He simply told his brother Bill to carry it as it would keep him safe while over there and that the Lord would be watching over him.

When the plane was getting ready to land at Cam Ranh Bay, Bill said "that it started feeling real when [our] plane was met by two fighter jets to escort [us] on to land." After they landed, they were issued their weapons and other gear. They were then loaded into Deuce and a Half trucks and trucked for a couple of hours to An Khe. He would spend thirteen days there, then at 0400 hours, they would be loaded into choppers, and all fourteen guys would be taken to Dak To.

The guys whom they were replacing, over half of them were wounded or dead. Bill talked to a guy named Lewis right after they got there because he was sitting in his foxhole, crying. When he asked what Lewis was crying about, Lewis said, "We were sent out here to die, and the C rations that we were given to eat are older than us." The C ration Lewis was holding was dated 1945, and Lewis was born in 1947; the C rations were WWII leftovers. Bill said that the whole time that they were there, they took a lot of incoming mortars and some rockets, but no attempt was ever made to overrun them. He contributed that to the presence of the ROK Marines. They were South Korean special forces soldiers located at Dak To with Bill's section. The Vietnamese feared them as they had basically no restrictions and were very brutal when fighting VC or NVA regulars.

In late April, Bill was sent to An Khe to take his GED test; he got loaded into the back a Deuce and a Half. As their convoy was headed through the An Khe pass, there was a huge firefight that they drove upon. It was between the First Infantry Division and VC. When the shooting ended, the convoy moved out; as they passed, Bill witnessed an old man pleading and begging for the soldiers to pay him for his water buffalo. It was lying on the road dead; it had been shot during the firefight. Lying next to the water buffalo in the ditch was a young girl who was also dead, shot in the head, more than likely the man's granddaughter. Half her head was missing. All the man cared about was getting paid for his water buffalo. That was just how that culture valued human life; it didn't have the same meaning to those people as it did to Americans.

Bill stayed at An Khe for a couple of days, took his GED test, and passed it. He was told that the results would be put in his file. When Bill got back home and got out of the military, there was no trace of it in his records. Bill would end up retaking the GED test and passing it at age thirty-two back in Ohio.

* * *

On May 23, Bill's section was sent to Buon Me Thuot. They were set up on a Q4 site, which was a radar that was part of rocket systems made for counterfire on incoming rockets and mortars. While there, his section had sixty-five confirmed kills on the enemy. At that site, Bill's section manned two radars and did all the forward observation for the counterfire. Shortly after Bill's section arrived at Buon Me Thuot, they started taking large amounts of enemy mortars and, occasionally, a rocket or two. The 173rd Airborne was called in to take care of the enemy activity in the area. The NVA was trying to overrun the outpost Bill's section was on.

During one of these exchanges with the enemy, Bill was performing duties as a forward observer when the outpost was almost overran. He called in illume rounds (this is a type of artillery round used to illuminate an area). When one of these illume rounds was fired overhead, a piece of the canister came out of the air and struck an ARVN (Army of the Republic of Vietnam) major that was standing beside Bill in the head. He dropped dead where he stood right beside Bill; there was nothing he could do for the major. The next five or six weeks after that attack, they kept getting mortared from a graveyard located in Buon Me Thuot, but it was off-limits from counterfire. This meant Bill's section was not allowed to engage them with artillery because the US was too afraid of the bad press and the negative effects it may cause with the civilian populace in the area. Finally, higher command gave the go-ahead for two gunship choppers to put an end to the threat. The chopper crews gladly obliged, and the threat was no more.

Shortly after this incident, Bill got to go up on a helicopter to retrieve a part for his section's radar. They would be flying from Buon Me Thuot to An Khe and back. When he was walking up to the chopper, he noticed the two-door gunners were picking up pieces of limestone the size of a man's fist out of the limestone helipad. They were piling them into the chopper by each gunner's area. He sat there with the gunners waiting for the pilots, for a while just shooting the shit with them. That was when he made a neat discovery: one of the door gunners was from Zanesville, Ohio. This was fascinating to Bill as it was a short twenty-minute drive from Coshocton, just across the county line in Muskingum County. They had a lot in common and even liked some of the same local bars and hangouts. It didn't take long, and the pilots showed up, and they took off. Soon, Bill found out what the pieces of limestone were for. As the chopper flew over the roads, they would get down to treetop level or even lower, and the gunners would hang out of their gun shoots and throw these fist-size limestone pieces at Vietnamese people on the road. Women, children, men—it didn't matter. They did not discriminate; a target was a target to them. It was a game they played; winning the hearts and minds of the locals they were not. These guys were all real assholes; they were completely crazy. Bill thought he couldn't wait to get off that chopper. On the way back to Buon Me Thuot with the part needed to repair the radar, they even flew so low over a guy who was in a small boat on the river below them that they prop washed him out of the boat. Bill said, "All the chopper pilots and door gunners [I] met over there were almost all completely crazy."

On August 18, not long after that ride, Bill would leave Vietnam and fly back to Fort Lewis, Washington. He remembered that buses came out on the tarmac to pick them up as they walked off the plane. This was because there were protesters everywhere inside the airport. Bill would then be flown to Columbus, Ohio, where he would only be greeted by his parents and taken home. This would wrap up Bill's active duty service with the army. He would be awarded the Vietnam Cross of Gallantry for his actions on this tour. Upon returning home, Bill would give his brother Jesse's Bible back and thanked him as he had returned home in one piece.

Bill put the army life behind him for years and became a family man until one day in 1990 when his older brother Jesse stopped by his house after one of his weekend drills with the Army National Guard. Jesse had some important news for Bill: he wanted to tell him that he was going to have to set this war out as Jesse's guard unit had gotten their alert order telling them they would be deploying to Iraq. At that moment, Bill thought, "Like hell I am"; so the next morning, he drove down to the recruiter's office in Coshocton and said he wanted to join and deploy with his brother. The recruiter told Bill he was too old; he was forty-one at the time. Bill would not take no for an answer. After a few minutes of persuading, the recruiter told Bill if he could lose six pounds by the following week, he would take him to MEPS in Columbus and see if the Guard would take him. Basically, he would have to pass their medical screening before being allowed to join back up. He lost the six pounds and went to MEPS and passed everything, so at forty-one, Bill was back in the military. He was ready to deploy with his brother Jesse and their unit to take on the Iraqi Army this time. Their unit would end up not being deployed to Iraq, and Bill would end up finishing that contract with the Guard honorably and got out when his four years were up.

SGT Roger Hill, Vietnam

September 1968–April 1970

In 1967, Roger went with longtime friend and neighbor Bill Maple to Fort Hayes in Columbus, Ohio, to join the army on the buddy program. They had gotten the idea after talking to a local recruiter about the buddy plan. Unfortunately, not long after they got to Fort Hayes, they figured out that wouldn't be the case. Roger was turned down because of his criminal record. Bill would join that day, and Roger would be sent home. This was a huge letdown for Roger as he had dropped out of high school to join. He wanted to go to Vietnam and follow his families' patriotic roots—his patriotic roots. Roger's father had served in WWII and his grandfather in WWI. However, just two weeks later, Roger would end up getting drafted anyway. He would be sent to Fort Jackson, South Carolina, for his basic training and then onto Fort Dix, New Jersey.

At Fort Dix, Roger would complete his infantry school and become an 11B (infantryman); he would then ship out for Fort Benning, Georgia, where he would do his airborne training.

After getting through all his training, he would end up getting stationed at Fort Bragg, North Carolina, as part of the Eighty-Second Airborne. He was there for a few months, and he thought he would never get to go to Vietnam. When most of his generation was running away from the war or at the very least hoping they would not be called upon, he was trying to go and couldn't. First, the army wouldn't take him; now, he was in the army's airborne infantry and still wasn't going. So Roger went to a recruiter in Fayetteville, North Carolina, outside Fort Bragg and signed up for another two years on his contract, which he was able to do since at the time he was a draftee. His plan worked; he was able to sign up, and now he was serving on his four-year total enlistment contract as a regular army soldier. Not long after that, in September 1968, Roger would get his wish and leave for Vietnam. He would be assigned to the 173rd Airborne Third Battalion C Company.

Roger was flown out by chopper to meet up with C Company, who was out in the bush on a thirty-day mission when he got there. He remembers jumping off that chopper to head across a rice paddy when he became stuck up to his waist in muck. At that same moment, gunfire erupted to his front. He thought, "I am a sitting duck out here." But no matter how hard he struggled, he was stuck in the middle of a field in the open. Just then, a couple guys ran over and, seeing him struggling, pulled him out of the muck. He would come to find out it was just a tiger, which was when Roger realized he had to be aware of everything; it was not just enemy soldiers that were trying to kill them. Vietnam was a dangerous place with unforgiving terrain, insects, plants, and wildlife that all could have deadly consequences as well.

When he arrived to his company's area, he was assigned to Charlie Company Third Squad. His new squad leader took one look at him and said, "What in the hell is in your ruck?" Roger took his ruck off for his new squad leader to go through. His new squad leader started tearing it apart. The first thing to go was half of Roger's food; he said, "You don't pack food for four days," which was how long they would go without resupply at a time when out in the field. "You only pack two days' worth. You are not going to have time to be lying around eating all day. This alone will lighten up your ruck a lot," he said. He also told him to only carry two quarts of water as they were in the mountains and good clean water was plentiful up where they were at. They were operating in the Central Highlands at that time, near the Bao Loc Pass. They also had him shed a few other nonessential items he had brought with him. This would hopefully keep him from sinking in the rice paddy again.

After squaring away Roger's gear, his new squad leader asked, "Hill, do you want to be an ammo bearer?" Roger thought for a second; if he wasn't shooting it, he sure as hell didn't want to have to carry it, so he replied no. Then the SSG (staff sergeant) asked, "How about RTO?" (That is the radio operator.) Roger said no again. Then the SSG asked, "Well, how about walking point man, then?" Roger replied, "Sounds good to me." He would continue this duty for the rest of his tour in Vietnam. "The average life expectancy of a point man in Vietnam when engaged during a firefight at the time was just seven seconds," Roger said.

The 173rd would be engaged with both North Vietnamese Army (NVA) regulars and Vietcong in brutal combat his entire tour. They would go out for thirty days at a time on what was known as search-and-destroy missions, also referred to as seek and destroy; they were just what they sounded like. They would patrol an area looking for the enemy, engage them when found, and destroy all assets they had as well.

At the time, the 173rd had no restrictions as far as ROEs (rules of engagement). This meant they could kill anyone they would see in this area of assignment. Of course, with ROEs like this, the fighting on both sides was even more brutal than you can imagine. The 173rd lost an entire platoon in Bravo Company to this brutal fighting; the NVA had overrun their position and killed all of them. They didn't stop there. They desecrated the entire platoon's bodies; they shot all of them in the head and cut off most of their fingers and other appendages. Roger said it was a horrifying sight and pissed off the entire brigade. Some of the soldiers would go on to repay the brutality by carving "173" in Vietnamese corpses with their knives after this incident to repay the favor and also to let the enemy know who was responsible for these deaths. They even went so far as to cut off the heads of NVA soldiers and hang them from their rucksacks in retaliation for what they did to Bravo Company. After that incident, no more prisoners would be taken by the 173rd.

It actually got so bad that their higher command decided to offer incentives for infantrymen out in the bush to start taking prisoners again. Higher command put out that any 173rd soldier to capture an enemy and bring them in alive would be given a three-day pass. Shortly after this, Roger was climbing down a very steep rock cliff when he saw a hole with a set of feet and a buttstock of a rifle sticking out. Normally, Roger would have thrown a hand grenade in the hole and would have been done with it. But that three-day pass was sounding pretty good. Roger decided to jump down with rifle pointed into the hole and surprise the VC, taking him prisoner. He would search him, and the VC only had one North Vietnamese dollar on him and an AK-47. Roger would keep that dollar and still has it to this day in a photo album in his home. This prisoner won Roger a three-day pass to Vung Tau, which is a peninsula east of Saigon on the coast. He said it was a great three days; he was able to meet a Vietnamese girl and rent a horse and buggy and take it all over the town on paved streets. He recalled all the people there were very nice and hospitable.

Roger also got a seven-day leave while he was there; it was sometime around March 1969. He went to Cam Ranh Bay, then would end up going to Saigon when he couldn't get a flight out of there. In his head, it was a good idea since the US embassy was there and he could get a passport and then get out of there. He ended up going out on the town that first night and was arrested by two MPs. They took him back and locked him up, as no 173rd soldiers were permitted in towns at that time. He would spend six days in that jail. He said it was hot, filthy, and just completely miserable in that jail.

The MPs would come in once a day, usually in the morning, and drag him out for questioning. It was always the same question, and they always got the same response. They would ask where he was from, and he would tell them the truth. They would tell him that they didn't have troops there and throw him back in his cell. After six days of this, they put him on a plane north to An Khe.

This was a long way from Bao Loc, so Roger had to hop rides and eventually got back to his company's area. Once back, he told a friend he had in the mail room to intercept anything that came in about that incident to his commander. Sure enough, a letter came in. Roger's buddy was true to his word, and the letter found its way into the trash. He thought he had gotten away with it until a few weeks later when he was told to report to the company commander's office. When Roger reported, his commander asked him what in the hell he was doing in Saigon. Roger was completely truthful with him, and the commander ended up just giving him a stern ass-chewing and sent him on his way.

Roger was walking point on one patrol when he noticed three armed Vietcong walking toward him. Roger stopped walking and put the lead VC in the sights of his M16. He shot him and dropped him in his tracks. The other two took off through the dense jungle, not to be found. Roger went up to the dead VC and picked up the SKS rifle the VC was carrying; he slung it on his back and took it with him back to their base camp. He would scratch "Bear Hill" into the buttstock so everyone else would know who it belonged to since he would be storing it in the platoon's conex. He would then do all paperwork to be able to keep it as a war trophy. Back in this time, you were able to do that with weapons as long as they were not full auto. Roger would have to keep that SKS in the platoon's locked-up conex until he went home on leave.

In October 1969, Roger got thirty days of leave between his first and second tour in Vietnam. Going home on leave was an adventure unto itself for Roger; he would fly out of Vietnam to Japan, where he had a few hours' layover. Roger found a couple of girls and was messing around with them when he realized he was late getting back for his flight. He hurried to get there; he made it just in time to watch his plane taxi off the runway and take off. He was stranded in Japan; it took him a while, but he was able to catch a military hop going to Travis Air Force Base in California. Then from Travis Air Force Base, he would hop on another flight to Fort Lewis, Washington. While he was at Fort Lewis, he had a little layover trying to get his tickets straightened out since he missed his flight in Japan. While he was doing this, his luggage was stolen. Roger would go the rest of his trip home with only the clothes on his back and the SKS he was carrying. He then was able to get on a civilian airliner and flew to Chicago, then onto Columbus, Ohio. He would call a taxi and take it for the eighty-mile ride back to West Lafayette, Ohio. He did all this while carrying his SKS war trophy that he took off the VC he shot. He said that the only time he had any issues doing this was on the flight from Washington to Chicago when he had to leave the SKS with the pilots in their cockpit until they landed and they handed it back to him. He said from Chicago to Columbus he just took it to his seat with him and no one said a thing. Roger has this SKS sitting in his house to this day.

Roger had a good time while home on this leave; he saw all his family and friends back home. Jesse gave his Bible to Roger during his leave as Bill Maple had the Bible on him during the same time that Roger was in Vietnam for this first tour. Bill had just returned in August from Vietnam. Jesse gave Roger this Bible and told him to carry it with him as Jesse and his brother Bill both had. Roger would end up carrying that Bible in a plastic bag in his right breast pocket from that day forward.

After the thirty-day leave, Roger went back to the same unit as before: C Company, Third Battalion, 173rd Airborne. He would be promoted to sergeant not long after he got back from that leave. He was a private first class when he first arrived in country and made specialist 4 and now sergeant. His new rank of sergeant meant increased responsibility as he was now in charge of other troops. He didn't let the promotion go to his head though. Even as a sergeant, Roger continued to walk point; usually this was not the case as they normally would have one of the lower-ranking guys walk point because of how dangerous it was. Roger didn't want to do that to any of his guys, and he said that to be completely honest, he didn't trust anyone else to do it. Also he kind of liked it, as crazy as that sounds. Roger said that he would never ask any of his men to do something that he wouldn't do himself. He had actually come to enjoy walking point man with a machete in his left hand cutting and hacking trail while holding his M16 in his right hand ready for action.

Shortly after that promotion, Roger's unit would be moved to Phan Thiet area, which was more of a sparsely vegetated area, an almost-desert area of Vietnam. He said this was quite a change; they were no longer fighting in the mountains that they all had become accustomed to. They now had to carry a lot more weight in their rucks since they had to pack all their water in on their backs. In the mountains, they would operate with two quarts of water on them; now they would carry twenty quarts on them for a four-day period.

During this time, Roger was walking point one day when he came across a bunker up ahead of him. It was the rear of a bunker. He thought he would just sneak up on that bunker and get a couple of kills to himself, loners so to speak. "Loners were very rare. They were bragging rights for an infantryman. You would have all the glory," Roger said. As Roger was edging up on the bunker, what looked to be a damn dinosaur came running up the path right at Roger. He had no choice but to shoot it. He killed it, but the bunker wound up being empty, so he lucked out there since he blew his cover shooting the dinosaur-like creature that charged him. With a little research, they identified the creature as a Komodo dragon; it was the first time anyone in his squad had ever seen one let alone been charged by one.

There were other times wildlife proved to be just as dangerous as the enemy. Roger recalled on his first tour, he was climbing down the rock face of a mountain when he felt something sting him. He looked down; it was a scorpion, and it had stung him on his arm. Since he was hanging onto a rock wall at the time, he couldn't swat it off himself. He turned to the guy with him and told him what had happened and that it was still on his ammo belt. He was able to remain calm and finish the climb down. He then shook off the scorpion and used the butt of his M16 to crush it. The medic was able to give Roger some sort of a shot for it. Roger said that later that night, they started getting mortared; and he started to hallucinate, thinking everyone was the enemy, and could not think clearly at all because of that scorpion sting. He wasn't right for quite some time after that; he believes he should have been sent to the rear for that sting, now looking back on the incident.

Another time, Roger said they had a close call with a giant snake while they were crossing a swamp. They came across an aggressive snake that was huge. He said three of them jumped on its back to try to hold it while their M79 grenadier shot it in the head with three of the shotgun-style buckshot rounds he carried with him. It took that many shots to kill it. No one had ever seen a snake that size before. It was as big as an anaconda, which weren't supposed to be in that region; but to this day, Roger still has no idea what kind of snake that was.

Another time, his platoon came out of the trees and was crossing a grassy opening in the jungle when someone pointed at a black cloud coming at treetop level right for them. It was a swarm of giant hornets. Roger described them as thousands of swarming hornets around six inches long apiece. His platoon had to act fast, so they popped off four or five smoke grenades. Everyone laid flat on the ground together, hoping it would work. "It did. They flew on past us. That was one scary moment for all of us," Roger said.

Roger said that after a while, they left the desert area for mountains again. This time, they would find themselves operating on the edge of the country and even into Cambodia, he believes. He said this was very rough country with a lot of thick bamboo. In some places, it was so thick you could not hack your way through it; you would be there forever trying. One time, his lieutenant said it was too thick and ordered everyone to wade through a creek that had about waist-deep water since they could make better time not having to fight the bush. Roger was point man, as usual when he heard a bunch of cracking and brush breaking in front of him up on the bank; there were definitely people coming toward them. Roger had to act quickly, as his squad's lives depended on him. He ripped off an entire magazine of his M16 into the bush toward the sound. He hit one of them, dropping them; it turned out to be a friend of Roger's from another squad in his platoon.

Roger was told by his lieutenant that everyone was in the creek. Here, one squad decided to not take the creek and to blaze their own trail. Roger felt horrible; he had hit his friend three times in his legs. His buddy would end up losing a foot because of it. Roger was trying to apologize to the guy when his buddy said, "Don't worry about it, shit happens." They sat there and smoked a joint. That was the first time Roger really smoked marijuana over there. The medic was pretty much out of morphine because they were taking so many casualties, so a lot of guys in Rogers's unit started using marijuana for pain and also to take the edge off mentally. The level of stress these guys were operating under daily were unimaginable to the average person, so they had to do something to take the edge off. This same time, the 173rd would have all alcohol taken away from their rations; up until this point, they were allowed a beer a day when they could get it from resupply. As Roger and his buddy sat there on the bank smoking that joint waiting for a medevac, his buddy said, "Don't worry about it. You just punched my ticket back to the homeland now." Roger said it was not uncommon for guys to be under so much stress over there that they would shoot themselves just so they could go home.

At one point during this tour, Roger's platoon was out on a thirty-day mission when a typhoon hit Vietnam. This storm would hit the coastal area hard and would halt resupply missions for quite some time. His platoon would end up having to stop hunting for enemies, and they started hunting for food—mostly some edible vegetation, birds, and orangutans. After about a week, the decision was made to start hiking out of the mountains back to base camp since the helicopters were not coming. On the way back, at the base of a mountain, Roger came upon a field of cabbages; he was starving, so he took his machete and hacked one off and ate it while walking out. He said that was a really bad decision; he shit like a goose for the next two weeks after that.

In the early summer of 1970, Rogers's second tour would come to an end as it was time for him to rotate back to the world (the United States) and so he could have some dwell time in garrison and also to go to his NCO (noncommissioned officer) school so he could make staff sergeant. He would be attending his NCO school at Fort Bragg, North Carolina, so his training unit would be the Eighty-Second Airborne. He remembers his first sergeant there hating on him because he was from the 173rd Airborne. It was basically a rivalry thing between the two.

Roger didn't adapt well to garrison life in the army. He needed to be out doing his job as an infantryman, not sitting around on an army post stateside "playing bullshit Mickey Mouse games all day." There was a war going on, and in Roger's mind, no one was acting like it back home at the time. Roger took it upon himself to leave and go home for the weekend to Ohio as he couldn't take much more of the games. This decision would cost him; he would end up missing an inspection that would have guaranteed him his SSG. The first sergeant on whose shit list Roger was already on called him at home in Ohio and asked him what the hell he was doing. Roger lied and told him his aunt had died. The first sergeant said he didn't give a shit and told him to report back immediately. Roger did and faced an Article 15 for his actions, plus his staff sergeant rank was as good as gone now. His fate was left solely up to his commander now.

When he got back to the Eighty-Second, his commander didn't do much, as Roger was the only combat-hardened infantry sergeant he had in his formation. The unit desperately needed his experience. He would have Roger teach weapons classes and other field craft classes to the troops to prepare them for Vietnam. This was not what Roger wanted to do at all. Luckily, a volunteer mission for 1,500 troops came down, and Roger signed up and was accepted. He was heading back; this time, he would be in the Second Battalion D Company of the 173rd. He would be assigned his own squad and would pick up where he had left off walking point. It was unheard of for a squad leader to come into country and take over walking point, but Roger liked it and also didn't trust anyone else with that responsibility.

It all happened so fast. Roger had actually forgotten to bring his field knife and the pocket Bible. He had mistakenly left them at his parents' house in West Lafayette, Ohio. Lucky for Roger, his mother and neighbor Mrs. Maple (Jesse and Bill's mother) kept in good contact. He said they would write multiple-page letters to him weekly the entire time he was in Vietnam. He said he would feel a little bad because he would only write back occasionally, and it would only be a paragraph at most when he did. Well, now Roger had something to write home for; he asked both of them to look through his things and to send him his knife and Bible. He felt like he was not complete with them missing, like something just wasn't right.

Not long into the third tour, Roger was preparing himself and others in his section to leave out on patrol when he tripped a booby trap and was blown apart. Shrapnel ripped through his body everywhere from head to toe. Roger remembers seeing a lot of other guys go down after being hit, and they all reacted differently. Some guys would go into shock after getting just a small wound. He always wondered how he would react if he got hit. Roger vividly remembers lying on the ground bleeding everywhere, dirt thick in his eyes. He still remembers spitting out the gum he was chewing and looking at his pinkie finger hanging from his hand, barely attached. He remembers thinking "They can just cut that off. I don't need it anyway."

Medics would work on him for forty-five minutes in the field while they were waiting for the medevac helicopter to get him out of the jungle. During these forty-five minutes, Roger could hear the guys around him talking about how messed-up he was. Roger told them to shut the hell up; he didn't want to hear any of that. Roger passed out for a while. When he came to, he was surrounded by a couple preachers, and they were reading his last rights to him. The medics actually had stopped working on him thinking he had died. He said he had been in a dream world where he was riding a big black stallion into a mountain range surrounded with tall grass. It was a breathtaking scene, almost like heaven. Roger actually believes he had died and was dead for a short time and that God decided it wasn't his time to go for whatever reason. He remembered thinking, "If this is what happens when you die, it isn't that bad." He soon found himself on the chopper headed to the Sixty-Seventh Evacuation Hospital. A door gunner kept shaking Roger to keep him awake and to try to keep him from going into shock. The gunner was Don Darr from Coshocton, Ohio.

Darr still remembers that day when he took the flight with Roger. Darr was sitting in the door gunner's seat, and they put a 173rd guy on the helicopter, who was really messed-up badly. Darr would keep reassuring him that he would be all right and that he was on his way back to the world (United States). At the time, Darr had no idea who Roger was, but he talked to him all the way back to the field hospital. Later, Darr would get a chance to talk to Roger back in the States at Valley Forge General Hospital in Pennsylvania. Darr said a bus came in, and he asked if anyone from the 173rd Airborne was aboard. One guy answered, and when Darr walked back, it was Roger. Don asked Roger where he was from, and Roger said he was from West Lafayette, Ohio. Don thought, *Oh my god.* He told Roger, "I am from Coshocton." It seemed crazy to both of them that they would run into each other like that in Vietnam when they lived in the same county probably less than ten miles apart from each other.

Roger would end up spending eight more months at Valley Forge General Hospital recuperating from his wounds. While re, Roger's knife and Bible would end up getting delivered to him in the mail one day. He was amazed they made it to him. He had written them off, figured he would never see them again. His mother had gotten his letter and mailed them to him in Vietnam; however, Roger had gotten blown up in the meantime.

Roger would end up discharging from the army at Valley Forge General Hospital in April 1971. He would receive two Bronze Stars, a Combat Infantry Badge, and a Purple Heart for his actions and service while in Vietnam.

Roger with his SKS that he brought home from Vietnam as a war trophy

SGT Cliff McPeak, Iraq

February 2003–June 2004

In 1970, Cliff would join the Ohio Army National Guard, and he would be assigned to the 214th Maintenance Company as a 63B light-wheeled vehicle mechanic. Cliff would spend six years in the Guard, and then he got out as he just had a lot of other stuff to occupy his time at that point in his life. After being out of the military for seventeen years, Cliff had a few buddies—Bill Maple, Jesse Maple, and Nick Davis—he let talk him into joining again in 1993. This came not long after a divorce, and Cliff was just looking for some comradery and something to do, really, at the time. He almost got out in 1995 when his second one-year enlistment was up. He was at a drill in civilian clothes turning in his gear when a sergeant major asked him why he was getting out. He let that SGM know some of his bitches and the complaints he had, and to make a long story short, that SGM was able to get him to reenlist and was able to get him to transfer units, which would eventually lead to Cliff finding a home in the 1485th Transportation Company, which would be out of his hometown of Coshocton. He would end up spending the last twelve years of his military career there.

Cliff worked at the county engineer's office as a highway maintenance worker with Jesse Maple. That was when Jesse and Cliff became really good friends. Cliff was also good friends with Jesse's brother Bill Maple. On February 9, 2003, Cliff's unit, the 1485th, was told that they would be mobilizing in support of Operation Iraqi Freedom. Cliff's father was on his deathbed that weekend, and his drill that month was the eighth and ninth. On Saturday morning, Cliff went downstairs in his uniform to tell his father he was leaving for drill. When his father heard this, his father just started shaking his head violently no, as he didn't possess the strength to talk anymore. He was refusing to let him leave. Cliff called the unit and was able to take that day off to be by his father's side. His dad ended up passing away later that day.

The next morning, Cliff went to drill, and that was when his unit was notified officially of their upcoming deployment around noon on February 9. They would be deploying in support of OIF1, which would be the main invasion of Iraq. Cliff went to work at his county job and told Jesse about the news of the upcoming deployment. Jesse told Cliff he had something for him. Jesse would end up going out to Cliff's home one evening and would hand him a small pocket Bible. He told Cliff to keep this Bible with him at all times and that the Lord would watch over him. He told him about the three guys who had carried it with them to Vietnam and back alive. Cliff accepted the Bible and would carry it in his left breast pocket for the entire deployment.

The 1485th TC would be leaving their armories in Coshocton and Dover, Ohio, to head to Fort Lee, Virginia, to mobilize. They would be at Fort Lee until April 2003. That was when they would fly out of Richmond, Virginia, for Kuwait. Once in Kuwait, the unit would have a little more training to go through and would have to get their trucks ready before heading north into war. The unit would send a few people north just days after they got in the country. Others would leave as needed in small groups. Cliff's turn to go north would come on June 29, 2003. He would leave Camp Victory, Kuwait, and head north to Camp Navistar, Kuwait, which was located on the border of Iraq, and stay overnight.

The next morning, on Cliff's fifty-third birthday, they crossed the border into Iraq and headed for Baghdad. President Bush had just declared Iraq as a victory and said all major combat operations were over. Cliff says he remembers thinking *bullshit* as he was driving by still-burning Iraqi tanks and other vehicles on the highway. He was thinking, *What in the hell have I gotten myself into?* as he passed those vehicles. After getting to Baghdad BIAP (Baghdad International Airport, to be more precise), once their tiny four-truck convoy arrived. They linked up with another convoy of 1485th TC soldiers and followed them back to Camp Anaconda, Balad, Iraq, which would become home to Cliff for the rest of his deployment. He remembers being there for at least two weeks until the rest of the unit finally got there. The company commander and first sergeant were the last two to arrive from Kuwait. Cliff said his maintenance warrant officer had been in charge of everything up until that point.

For the next six months, they were running day convoys, which meant they would be there and back in the same day. They went from Camp Anaconda to BIAP normally, sometimes other FOBs (forward operating base) as well. Cliff was on most of these convoys, usually as the driver or assistant driver of the wrecker, which would normally be the second to last vehicle on the convoy. They normally had one gun truck behind them, providing rear security. Cliff said the majority of these convoys were pretty uneventful. On one convoy, he recalled they lost their rear gun truck to a breakdown. The rest of the convoy went ahead to a rally point and waited for them. They were able to get the truck hooked up to the wrecker and caught up with the convoy. "It was pretty nerve-wracking as you would have to get out of the wrecker and hook up the towing equipment from the wrecker to the other vehicle." While you did this, you would have to rely completely on your battle buddies to provide security for you. The standard unit maintenance protocol at the time was five minutes; that is the time they would have to make the repair. If it was estimated to take longer, you were supposed to hook it up to a wrecker and tow it. Every second that convoy was stopped, you were a target of opportunity for the bad guys. That is why being proficient at your job was so important.

Another convoy that sticks out to this day in Cliff's mind was when laziness of one of the truck drivers cost the unit dearly. The unit's policy was, after every convoy, the truck drivers would go to the fuel point and fill up their trucks; that way, they would be full for the next mission. So on a convoy to BIAP, they had a tractor go down when Cliff started his five-minute checks. The driver told

Cliff that he didn't know what happened, but after a minute or two, Cliff realized the truck had run out of fuel in the first tank. The driver then switched it to his second tank, but by this time, his truck, being diesel, had lost its prime and would not start. Of course, the driver had already run his batteries dead trying to start the truck before maintenance got there.

By the time Cliff figured all this out, his five minutes were long gone and a large crowd of Iraqis were starting to gather. He should have hooked it right then, but he continued to try to prime the truck by hand. Eventually, after ten minutes had gone by and the crowd was starting to get a little hostile, his sergeant first class told him to hook it up to the wrecker and get the hell out of there as their entire convoy was in jeopardy. Cliff scrambled and got the tractor hooked up to the tow bar that was on his tractor. The wrecker that they normally were assigned to was getting a new engine installed back at Camp Anaconda. Under the stress from the crowd and a different vehicle than he was used to working out of, Cliff didn't hook up the air lines from his tractor to the tractor they were going to tow. This saved them precise time in the danger zone, and he figured they didn't have a real long way to go and that when they got to BIAP, they could get it running from there.

The convoy took off once Cliff had everything hooked up and back in his truck. They were running probably 55 mph when, out of nowhere, the truck in front of Cliff's came to an abrupt stop. Cliff stood on his breaks, locking them up. However, the weight of the truck that he was towing was too much, and it continued to push him, causing a four-vehicle pileup. No one was seriously injured, but four vehicles were seriously damaged. An accident investigation followed. Cliff admitted he was in the wrong and explained why he did what he did. Everything was understood by the investigating officer, and Cliff was not charged for the damages. Cliff said, "They almost charged the lazy-ass truck driver who caused the whole thing by not topping off his fuel tank, but they didn't." No one would be faulted, and it would be written off as the risk of operating in a combat theater.

While in Iraq, the 1485th TC would be mortared or rocketed four or five nights a week. Normally, they wouldn't hit anything. However, one night, they were hit by a rocket attack, and a nineteen-year-old airman working right across from the 1485th's motor pool was killed. The US's counterfire was swift. The barn that the rocket had been fired from was leveled by US fire; nothing was left standing.

Another time, Cliff had just left the motor pool area to go to the main PX (post exchange) when a midday rocket attack happened. Al-Qaeda had brazenly fired twenty-one rockets into Camp Anaconda at one time, some of which landed in the 1485th's motor pool right where Cliff had been working, damaging a trailer that he had just been working on. Cliff believes God was looking out for him, and he was at the PX when this happened.

Regarding creature comforts or lack thereof, Cliff said he didn't get a shower for a month at a time. They were just using bottled water to bathe with. He would use two large bottles at a time for bathing and would also wash his clothes that way. He would just use a large pan to wash them in. During this time, they were living in tents with dirt floors and no AC. After about three months in Iraq, the engineers finally got to the 1485th's stuff, and they got showers and wood flooring built for their tents. Also, they got AC in their tents. Cliff was very grateful for this, although it was ironic that it was around September and the 130°F-plus days were behind them. He also could remember how happy their unit was when they started getting four bags of ice a day for their entire 175-person unit.

Cliff would get to go home for a two-week leave in October, but he had mixed feelings about going back. He felt like he belonged over there doing his duty and didn't want to leave his fellow soldiers. This was what he had signed up to do. The unit actually ended up with one fatality, and it was a soldier on leave. A nineteen-year-old soldier died in a car accident while home on his two-week leave.

On one of the unit's last missions, they took enemy fire, small arms and RPGs (rocket-propelled grenades). One of their trucks was hit by an RPG, and it creased the fuel tank and then hit the frame rail and blew a perfect hole through it. When it exploded, it took out all the airlines, a lot of electrical wires and blew two tires out. This was Staff Sergeant Beal and Staff Sergeant Kula's truck. They were able to drive it out of the kill zone and to the rally point up the road. Maintenance looked at it, and it would not be repairable.

The 1485th TC was supposed to leave Iraq on April 14; however, due to the roads being black because of the threat level, they wouldn't actually leave until April 16. They convoyed all their equipment back to Kuwait. When they got to Kuwait, they power washed all their equipment and prepared it to go back to the States. After about two weeks in Kuwait, they flew out to Ireland for their plane to refuel. While it was refueling, the troops partook in a few drinks at the bar in the terminal to celebrate a successful deployment. After two hours or so, they got back on the plane and headed for Virginia and back to Fort Lee to demobilize, which took them a week. Then they flew back to Ohio on a C-135 back to Mansfield, Ohio. Cliff remembers this because he was chosen, for some reason, to sit in the cockpit; it had a third seat that was open just behind the pilot and copilot, and that was where he was able to sit.

After his leave was over and he returned to work at the Coshocton County Engineer's office, he gave the Bible back to Jesse because he said he needed to pass it on to another local guy who had just gotten his mobilization orders for Iraq.

After the war, Cliff would go on to serve another three years in the Ohio Army National Guard and would retire in 2007 with twenty years and one month of service.

SPC Zac Miller, Iraq

October 2004–January 2006

In May 2004, I was serving in the Ohio Army National Guard when my unit received its warning order that said we would be deployed in the fall with the 101st Airborne to Iraq. Since 9/11 happened, I was eager to get into the fight, as were most of my friends in the unit. After all, this was what I signed up for when I was still a junior in high school. In 2000, at the age of seventeen, Jared Lillo and I had signed up on the buddy plan and went to basic training the summer between our junior and senior years in high school. This was what was known as the Split Option program back then, as you would return from your basic training and go back to high school for your senior year. During this time, you would be doing your weekend drills with your guard unit and receiving drill pay, so it was a great way to make money as a high school student. And the way I looked at it, I was getting a year toward my retirement goal while still in high school. It was a win-win for me, as I already knew I wanted to be a career soldier.

I was seventeen then; now, at the age of twenty-one, I wanted to prove myself. I knew this would change me for the rest of my life, if by no other way than giving me the privilege of wearing that coveted right sleeve patch. Army soldiers who are deployed to a combat zone get authorized to wear it for the rest of their careers. This patch is a lot of times referred to as a combat patch. Really, it just should be called a "deployment to a combat zone" patch, but that doesn't sound as good, I guess. Back then, there were only a handful of soldiers who had a patch on their right sleeve, most of which had served in the first Gulf War in 1990–1991 and a few were crusty Vietnam vets. As a young troop, these were the guys whom you looked up to. They were the only real vetted soldiers in our ranks who had been there and done that. I was ready to become one of them. I wanted to prove my worth as a soldier and do my duty across the pond on the two-way rifle range.

My right sleeve combat patch earned on my first deployment

Living in a small community in the Appalachia part of Ohio means news travels fast. My father was an Air Force and Army National Guard veteran and was good friends with Jesse Maple, whom I knew as well. When Jesse heard the news, he contacted my father and asked him to have me stop by his house because he wanted to talk to me. Jesse was sort of a locally known legend in the local veteran community. He was known as a soldier who was tough as nails and didn't have the word *quit* in his vocabulary, exactly who I would have wanted by my side in a firefight. So when I heard this, I went to his house and met him for a sit-down talk. I didn't really know what he was going to tell me, but I figured it would be good knowledge I might be able to use. It turned out he wanted to give me his tattered Bible to carry so that it may somehow help protect me as it did all the soldiers in the past who had carried it and came home alive. I graciously accepted the gift and felt honored to be among this short list of true American patriots to have carried it into harm's way.

A few weeks later, on October 30, 2004, my unit left Ohio for the mobilization site, which would be Camp Atterbury, Indiana. This would be home for the next few months while we trained in the snow for a war we would fight in the desert. Literally, we were training in six inches or more of snow in December; this is a prime example of army logic at its best. Our unit had a four-day pass over Christmas, and then we had to be back at Camp Atterbury to ship out. Our unit would fly out of Indianapolis, Indiana, for Germany, then onto Kuwait. When I was headed onto the tarmac to board the jet, a group of Gideons were handing out pocket Bibles to those of us who would accept one. I took one and tucked it into the breast pocket of my uniform in the same plastic bag that Jesse's Bible was in.

On December 28, 2004, we landed in Kuwait. I will never forget that day. Stepping off the plane into the heat of the desert was a weird feeling, almost as weird as stepping off a commercial plane in full kit, including gas mask and weapon. All that we didn't have on us at the time was ammo. As any good soldier would be thinking, I was wondering, *When in the hell am I going to be getting my ammo issued?* As we got loaded onto buses on the tarmac, I was given a single thirty-round magazine for my M16 and told to load it. We would not be issued our full combat load of ammo for a few days. A combat load of ammo for an M16 or M4 is 210 rounds of ammo. At the time, the policy was that we would carry two combat loads of ammo on us in Iraq. As a SAW (squad automatic weapon) gunner, a double combat load would be 1,600 rounds. Kuwait at the time was relatively safe; the threat level was not as high as it was in neighboring Iraq, where we would be in a little over a month. When on post inside the wire, we were only required to carry one thirty-round magazine with us. A SAW gunner would have to carry a minimum of a hundred linked rounds on post. Off post outside the wire was where we had to have two combat loads with us.

I was a 45B at the time—present-day 91F—which is a small arms / artillery repairer. In civilian terms, I was a gunsmith who worked on weapons ranging from handguns all the way up to mortars and towed artillery. Being that I was very proficient with all weapons systems, I was picked to be a gunner for convoys and any recovery missions my section would be called for. I carried an M249 SAW, which stands for squad automatic weapon It is a belt-fed 5.56mm. I would only have to carry the SAW when outside the wire though. I was able to retain my M16 still for when I was on post, which was a big win in my book. I was lucky I didn't have to lug the SAW around every day as some soldiers had to. I was in an MST (maintenance support team) section. Maintenance support teams at the time were made up of one armament repairer (which was me), one welder, one electronics repairer, a generator mechanic, and a few wheeled vehicle mechanics and at least one of them had to be H8 qualified—that is the mechanic who runs the wrecker. This was why our section was so valuable. We could fix, recover, or lift about anything you would have in a normal unit.

In late January 2005, we convoyed from Camp Virginia, Kuwait, to Camp Anaconda, Iraq. This was a two-day convoy during the rainy season. It was pouring rain the first day and night of our journey, enough that everything flooded. Our trucks were all hillbilly armored: sandbags on the floors and welded plate steel on the doors. We had no widows in our trucks; they were all removed so the plate steel could be welded and hung in place. We had a quick safety brief and a review of our ROEs (rules of engagement), which, at the time, stated that we pretty much had to be shot at to return fire. Only exceptions were, if the person was carrying an RPG or if you observed them pointing a weapon at you or other troops, you could just shoot them on sight. In these rules, there was an escalation of force that we would all have to be proficient with. If you as the soldier messed these up, you would be prosecuted and could end up in jail. War has evolved on our side to be very politically correct. If you were wondering, the enemy doesn't abide by any of these rules.

After our convoy brief, it was off to our trucks to start our journey north into Iraq. I loaded up in the truck with my M249 and 1,600 rds of ammunition. I was nervous and figured that there was a good chance I wouldn't make it back. I grabbed my Bibles in my pocket and said a quick prayer to God and asked him to watch our six. That first day was miserable. It was cold and wet, not what I was thinking it would be like in the desert, but I guess in January this was normal in Kuwait and Iraq. We did have to recover a few of our trucks that got stuck in the sand, which had turned into a glue-like substance with all the rain we had gotten. I was glad I was a gunner at these times. I just had to pay attention and provide over watch. Jared Lillo, who had joined the military with me four years earlier, was one of the wrecker operators in my unit. He was in MST 2 and I was in MST 4, so we were in the same platoon but different sections. Our mechanics would have to get out of their vehicle and either fix the broken-down vehicle immediately or, in most cases, just hook it up and tow it to the next FOB where it could be fixed inside the wire.

The second day was very eventful. Somewhere in the middle of nowhere, in the desert in Southern Iraq, I saw my first Iraqi carrying an AK-47. He was walking against the direction of our convoy, with the AK-47 slung facing down. We kept rolling. I just kept eyes on him, and my weapon was ready, safety off. We passed with no event. A few hours later that day, we were approaching Baghdad, which we were going to skirt around so we would not have to go through some of the most dangerous routes in Iraq at the time. I was in the third vehicle from the rear of our convoy. Our convoy was probably about thirty vehicles in this one as it was about one-third of our entire unit's equipment. We started to see our unit's trucks passing us in the lane coming toward us and came to find out our lieutenant leading the convoy was lost. There is an old joke that goes around in the army that you can't spell lost without an LT. This seems to be a very accurate joke. He had read his map wrong and took our thirty-truck convoy on the wrong route through Baghdad instead of around. He then took us on a one-lane dirt road to reroute us back to the MSR (main supply route) we were supposed to be on.

About half a mile down this one-lane road in the middle of a populated area with people all around, we met another convoy. It was a transportation company of tractor trailers coming the other way at a one-lane bridge. All I could figure was, their lieutenant must have been lost as well. The TC company was crossing the bridge first; we had no choice but to pull over as far as we could and let them pass. Our spacing was all messed up and was a soldier's worst nightmare, as we were in the middle of town with people walking between our vehicles so close we had to yell at them for touching our vehicles. I still remember the face of one kid whom I yelled at for walking up against our truck. He stuck out to me because he was whiter than me and with blue eyes and light-blond hair. He appeared to be around fourteen or fifteen years old, I would estimate. I would never see another blond-haired civilian living in Iraq again. I remember telling some of the guys in my unit about it. I asked them if they thought he was a war baby from the first Gulf War in 1991. He was about the right age since it was now 2005.

I had an uneasy feeling inside me as we sat along that road. I could feel it deep down inside me that something bad was about to happen. Just about then, a tractor trailer from the TC company that was passing us went off the road and crashed down a steep embankment. Our unit's wrecker along with the TC unit's wrecker were able to flip it over and recover it. This all took time, though, and just as they finished with the recovery, within minutes, all the local people just disappeared. I didn't see anyone run or anything. Literally, they all just kind of slipped away. The bustling area was now desolate with no one in sight. No more did we realize this when we heard a deafening blast from an explosion at the rear of our convoy just two trucks back. It was an IED (improvised explosive device), more than likely a 155mm artillery round buried a little too deep to be effective. At that same time, our rear gun truck took small arms fire from their rear. They had an M2 .50 caliber machine gun on their truck, and they quickly silenced the threat, tearing one of the insurgents completely in two. None of us were hurt during that attack, thank God. That got all our attention; now we were all on edge and figured this was what we were in for the rest of the year.

We ended up making it to Camp Anaconda later that day. It seemed pretty nice. We had been there all of about twenty minutes when we had a mortar attack. Welcome to Mortaritaville, as some people joked. Camp Anaconda was known for being a favorite target for anti-American terrorists to fire on. That was how it got its nickname, Mortaritaville. During our time there, I put a tick mark on the blank page in the back of my Bible for each time we had a mortar or rocket attack on Camp Anaconda. I ended up with 194 ticks in the back of my Bible. I am sure I missed a few as I would occasionally sleep through them; after we were there a while, you become complacent to them. I have not been able to find any exact data to date how many actual impacts we had on our post. But if you google Mortaritaville, Wikipedia says the area received approximately seven hundred mortar impacts during my time there, so take that for what it is worth.

Once we arrived at Camp Anaconda, my section, MST 4, was split from our unit and assigned to a transportation battalion elsewhere in the 129th Logistics Task Force (101st Airborne) to help them with their maintenance and recovery needs. I enjoyed this, as my daily jobs were constantly changing. I obviously repaired any broken weapons as my first priority, but that was only enough work for maybe one day a week average. I volunteered for tower guard a lot and spent countless hours sitting on the perimeter, guarding the post. As I already stated, I was a gunner on a gun truck when needed, such as if our section got a call to go recover a blown-up or broken-down vehicle. Also, my parent unit, the 211th SMC (support maintenance company), was still on the same camp as my section, so I would occasionally go on convoy security missions with them whenever they were short of people. This happened a lot during the middle of deployment when our unit started rotating people home for their two-week leave. All the remaining time I spent working on vehicles in my section's maintenance bay even though I was not a wheeled mechanic. It was war, and all hands were on deck when we needed to get something done. I always placed the mission first. Sometimes I would have a crazy additional duty, like morgue duty, since I was a lower enlisted at this time. Morgue duty was a duty I will never forget. It was a very humbling experience.

Me providing convoy security as a gunner

I will never forget one of the close calls I had with a few mortar rounds while driving on post. It was in early July 2005. I remember this because it was right after my twenty-second birthday. Our section had just fixed a Humvee, and I was road testing it with one of the other guys in my section. We were going down the main drag of Camp Anaconda between the wash racks and the transient tents that troops would stay at when they were waiting to fly in or out of theater. These tents were not hardened as a lot of stuff on the camp was with T walls, sandbags, or HESCO barriers around them. So they were a perfect target for indirect fire. I heard a *boom* followed by another and another. I think it was on the third one that I finally saw impact and debris fly up. I was driving right toward it. I stopped. One impacted the roadway probably seventy-five yards in front of our vehicle.

They were walking the rounds into the transient tents on the edge of the airfield. Three or four more hit out toward the tents. A few parked vehicles sustained damage, and the wash rack was blown apart. Other than that, I don't think much damage was inflicted. That was a rare occurrence though. They had fired roughly ten rounds in on us; they hardly ever did that. Normally, they would fire one or two rounds at a time because we had such precise counter fire. If they fired more than once, we would normally be able to put rounds back on them. Camp Anaconda had such good counter fire that Al-Qaeda adapted to firing one or two rounds from mortar tubes that they would set up in the back of pickup trucks. They would drive parallel with the base and fire from the trucks while moving so we would not be able to counter effectively. I was told they would also set the mortar tube up with a block of ice in the tube and the round on the other side. When the ice melted, the round would drop and fire. When we would counter fire, no one would be there except an unmanned mortar tube to get blown apart. These tactics were not very effective, but with our camp being so large, they were able to harass and disrupt normal day-to-day life for us. They did occasionally get lucky and kill or wound some of us, but it was very rare. After you are on ground for a month or so, you become numb to the mortar and rocket attacks and just go about your day like nothing is up. I think we all just came to terms that if it was our day to die, it was our day. God would look out for me. We wouldn't even get out of our bunks at night after the first month or so to go to the bunkers. Usually, you would get up, throw your gear on, and run to a bunker just to get there and sit for thirty minutes when they only fired two rounds in on us and they exploded before you even knew what had happened.

One of our towers at Camp Anaconda, Iraq

One day I will never forget was when I was on tower guard with Scott Ball from Newark, Ohio, in tower 14 when Anaconda Main came over the radio and said for towers 14, 15, and 16 to button down the hatches as there was a 500 lb bomb getting dropped at azimuth such and such, danger close. I looked at Scott, and when we checked the azimuth that was drawn out on our tower's range card, we looked at each other and said almost in unison, "It is that mud hut directly in front of us 250 yards out." *Awesome, we had front row seats*, we both thought. Anaconda Main had radioed it would be dropped in five minutes. Well, a jet dropped it less than a minute after the radio transmission, and it was a direct hit. The mud hut was no more; all that was left was a smoking crater in the ground with debris scattered everywhere around it. We came to find out that a thermal surveillance camera that was mounted on one of the towers had caught an Al-Qaeda mortar team fire on our post and then pack up and head into that mud hut earlier that morning. They had been monitoring the hut to make sure no one left, and I guess the best solution was a 500 lb. bomb. I think it was a very fitting solution. Just one less mortar team we had to worry about in the future.

While I am on the subject of tower guard and Scott Ball, I am reminded of probably the maddest I had ever been while on deployment. Scott and I were on one of our mind-numbing five-hour shifts, of which we would do two in every twenty-four-hour period. So needless to say, we got to know each other pretty well. We also got to know the locals whom we observed every day. There was this one asshole of a kid who would herd sheep by our tower multiple times a day. He was probably twelve years old, give or take, and didn't like Americans, to say the least. He would normally just flip us off as he passed or possibly yell random cuss words at us in perfect English. But on this particular day, as he was passing by just outside the wire from us, he looked us in the eyes and yelled "Fuck you, Americans!" while pointing at a random sheep in the middle of his flock. He beat it in the head with his staff repeatedly. The sheep ran among the rest of the herd to try to blend in with the other sheep in hopes of getting away. It didn't work; he picked it out as he ran after it through the herd. With another swift hit, the sheep dropped lifeless. He turned and looked up at us and pointed at the sheep. He then said, "Fuck you.

This should be you." The rest of his herd just ran ahead of him to escape the madness.

Me with my M249 while on tower guard

Scott and I both had our weapons pointed at him, but we couldn't do anything to him. There was absolutely nothing we could do to this little shit. We were separated by a chain-link fence and ten feet of concertina razor wire. Furthermore, if he wanted to beat and kill his sheep and just leave him lying about in the desert, that was his prerogative, and we could not tell him otherwise. This was not the norm. The majority of the locals we had good relationships with. The adults usually went about like we didn't exist, and the kids of all ages either begged for stuff relentlessly from us or tried to barter with us in some way. They loved Red Bull, Coke, Pepsi, candy, and pretty much any type of Lickee's & Chewy's that us troops may have on us. The MREs (Meals, Ready to Eat) or a bottle of water that we would give them most of the time would be rejected, pretty much the same way a private in the army would do. Privates will only eat MREs and drink water if they are made to by their leadership or if it is their last resort. In their defense, some of the MREs are pretty damn bad.

Believe it or not, probably the closest to death that I ever came was not from an enemy bullet, mortar, rocket, or IED explosion. It was from a burst of a machine gun from a battle buddy who was in my section. After our section got assigned to the TC unit as their MST, we moved over to trailers to live. They were like house trailers with three rooms in them. They had three twelve-by-twelve-foot rooms in them with doors that faced outward. They were all two-man rooms. My roommate and I were awakened one night by the deafening sound of a machine gun going off. When I opened my eyes in terror, the room was pitch-black except for the muzzle flashes. While still lying in bed, I grabbed my rifle that was beside me and racked a round into my chamber. Jimmy, my roommate, had not said a word or made a movement yet. His bed was on the side of the room that the machine gunfire was coming from. Upon hearing my M16 chamber a round, out of the dark came Jimmy's voice. "Miller, are you hit?" I answered "No, are you?" as I was getting up. I turned the light on, and we realized the thirty rounds or so that was fired had been fired from our battle buddy's room, who will remain nameless for this story.

I ran next door and threw open his door expecting the worst. But what I saw when I went through the door was my buddy holding his M249 with a two-hundred-round drum still loaded standing in shock in the middle of his room dressed in nothing but his underwear. He had apparently left his loaded machine gun lying on his bed and went and got drunk, which we weren't allowed to do. Then when he came back, he decided to strip down to his underwear in the dark and climb into bed. That was when he thought it would be a good idea to pick up his SAW by the pistol grip and, apparently, the trigger, which sent a large burst through his bed and our wall. Talk about an adrenaline rush. Holy shit, that had us going. I took the SAW from him, unloaded it, and we all just went back to bed. The neighboring Joes never did find out what the hell happened. We just played it off as we didn't know either. At 0200 hours, no one really gave a shit, I guess. We went back to bed, and the next day, we were able to procure a mattress and a couple of area rugs for each room to lay over the bullet holes. No one ever did get in trouble over that incident. I still can't believe the area rugs worked.

From all the dangers that we faced that year, my unit deployed 211 troops and returned with 210. We only had one death among our ranks. That came in the form of a noncombat-related death. SFC Daniel Pratt passed away. He was a section sergeant for one of the other MSTs in my platoon. I believe it was determined a heart attack. This shows just how unforgiving the heat and environment over there was. It was nothing for the temperatures to be well above the 120°F mark. I think the highest I ever saw that I can remember was 138°F. This mixed with high levels of stress, both mental and physical, proved to be a deadly combination. You could not take a day off if you were not feeling well or if it was too hot. We were in a war. You just had to wear your body armor and full kit in the heat and do your job no matter what because your brothers and sisters to your right and left were depending on you. It is this way in all wars; the elements that soldiers face are a lot of times as dangerous, if not more dangerous, than the enemy we are there to fight. We lost another soldier from that deployment shortly after returning home. He committed suicide as he was trying to patch his life back up after deployment, and the stress became too much for him to handle.

SGT Zac Miller, Kuwait

January 2008–January 2009

It had been two years since my last deployment to Iraq, almost to the day when my new unit got mobilized in support of Operation Iraqi Freedom. This time, I was a sergeant in the 134th Field Artillery (FA) SVC Btry. We would mobilize as an infantry brigade combat team (IBCT). Ohio's IBCT was the Thirty-Seventh, which, back in WWII, was known as the Thirty-Seventh Division. We would be three thousand troops strong and would deploy into theater to run all security theater-wide. The Thirty-Seventh would put an infantry battalion in Iraq along with the cavalry battalion. The other infantry battalion would be stationed in Kuwait and run gun truck escort missions into Iraq, some lasting thirty days at a time. The 134th FA, which was my battalion, would be in charge of all security in Kuwait. The support battalion would be scattered about as needed throughout theater. That was how the stage was set for my 2008 deployment. The Buckeye Brigade, as the Thirty-Seventh is known, would be running operations.

I left Jesse's Bible at home this time, as I didn't know if it could withstand another trip to the sandbox. The years in the jungles with the monsoons and the deserts with the extreme heat and sands had not been kind to it. So this trip, I opted to only take my own pocket Bible, the one that I had carried the entire first deployment in a plastic bag with Jesse's Bible cover to cover. I made it back in one piece, and I figured whatever luck that Bible of Jesse's had surely had to rub off. That's what I believed anyway. I believed, as every soldier that had carried it into battle so far did, that when you had it with you, God was watching over you.

One of the two infantry battalions our brigade had would be used in Iraq for area and base security along with the cavalry battalion. The other infantry battalion would be used for convoy security missions going from Kuwait up into Iraq and back. The field artillery battalion I was part of left their howitzers back in Ohio and was basically used as another infantry battalion doing area security and base security. So much for being king of battle, I guess.

My small but important piece of the equation was as truck commander and later on deployment NCOIC (noncommissioned officer in charge) as QRF (quick reaction force) team at the SPOD (sea port of debarkation), previously known as Camp Spearhead. I earned this position because I was one of the few guys who had combat experience in the unit at the time. I was marked by my right sleeve combat patch. I was starting to become one of those crusty old guys whom I used to look up to when I was a young troop. The SPOD is the sea port where everything came in and out of theater at the time, at least rolling stock as it was a deep-water port.

As QRF, our job consisted of fence line checks at least two times during our twelve-hour shift. We would check every inch of fence line inside and out with a drive-by inspection. This also was a show of force to help deter any threats, as we would be in our up-armored Humvees with gunners up in the turrets and machine guns mounted and loaded. We would also be tasked with driving all three of the piers and calling in any changes of vessels that were in port. This was also a show of force on the piers by having up-armored Humvees with machine guns mounted and gunners up in the turret. These were our daily duties. We would always be on call as well for any issues that would pop off in our area of operation. We were the first line of defense and also backup to anyone who had an issue in our area of responsibility. This would include searching and detaining suspected terrorists and investigating threats that were called in by our soldiers at all of our ECPs (entry control points). Our unit was in charge of two search pits, and we would help search trucks on large convoys and provide overwatch on all the TCNs while this was happening. This was a great assignment, and looking back on it, I would say it was my funniest year and also the most rewarding year of my military career.

Me and SPC Lawrence inside of our QRF gun truck

I will give you a quick comparison of how stuff had changed since my first deployment. My first deployment ammunition was pretty much a free-for-all. I had over two thousand rounds of ammunition. I even had three grenades that had just been handed to me by a Joe who was getting ready to leave theater and who didn't need them anymore. I still remember what he told me. He said, "Here, I hope you get a chance to use these. I carried the damn things around all year and never got to set one off." Unfortunately, I never did either, and I passed them on to another new guy when I left theater. That was 2004–05, and things were different back then. Now in 2008, we stored our weapons inside an arms room and were issued them before leaving the wire for duty every day. We were also issued our ammo and signed for it daily for all our weapons systems. This meant—you guessed it—we had to sign it all back in after every twelve-hour shift. If you were short even one round, a report had to be made. If you just lost it, you would receive an Article 15 and would lose pay or have extra duty, whatever your chain of command decided. This is the army for you. The war was won; now we were just trying to nation-build and keep the peace. This means stupid shit like this was being made up for the troops to do by the higher-ups with too much idle time on their hands.

As QRF, there was never a dull moment. One night, not long after getting in theater, we were called to one of our ECPs (entry control points) that was out on one of the piers. The personnel there had searched a driver entering the controlled pier to access a US Navy vessel that was in port. They had taken a cell phone off him and then granted him access. The cell was taken because it was a camera phone, and they did not allowed cameras in the area. Well, our guards were creeping on this TCN's (third country national) phone when they realized that in his videos and pictures were dead American soldiers. He had a few videos with footage of American convoys being blown up and soldiers being killed. It appeared that these were not downloaded but recorded with this phone. So my truck was sent over to confirm what our gate guards had called in on the radio and to detain the TCN. Upon arrival, we took the phone and verified that, indeed, the guards were accurate in their reporting. We had to go onto the ship and detain the TCN. We searched him and pulled over $1,000 off him and also some Kuwaiti dinar—I don't remember how many, but the stack was quite impressive. He had nothing else of significant value or interest on him. We placed him in black plastic flex cuffs that we carried and waited for our interpreter to get there. We knew he could speak English, but he was staying tight-lipped. Once the interpreter got there, it was more of the same, so we called in KCID, which I believe to be similar to the FBI in the United States. I will never forget this as long as I live. These two guys rolled up to our location in a white Suburban, both dressed in bright-white man dresses and aviators. One was very heavyset, my guess is 5 feet, 5 inches, 350 lb, and the other guy was like 6 feet and 120 lb soaking wet. It was a completely ridiculous sight. They had guns and other gear, but it was all just lying about in their Suburban. They talked with us a little and took the statements that we had prepared for them and all the evidence we had collected and put it in their vehicle, then walked over to the TCN and said maybe five words to him in Arabic. The guy immediately broke down sobbing uncontrollably and was shaking in fear. They took him away, and we never saw him again. I asked our local interpreter what was going to happen, and he said zero tolerance and that they were probably going to execute him.

Detaining people was at least a weekly event. Usually it was over stupid stuff, like taking unauthorized pictures. Pictures of the port or of any of the base were not allowed, as they could be used as planning tools for the enemy to plan for an attack or just for the enemy to gather other small pieces of information that may be used against us. We would usually give the person a choice if it appeared to be a harmless incident. We would give them the choice of giving us the camera, and we would check the pictures. This was easy, as the majority of the cameras we encountered were digital types with a screen on which we could view all pictures on the camera's memory card. We would delete any unauthorized pictures, escort them out of our area, and give them the camera back. If they refused, they would be detained, and we would remove the camera from their possession.

One incident we were called to take care of was when a TCN was spotted on the pier taking pictures of an American vessel that was in port unloading its cargo. When we got to him, he was still taking photographs of our ship, and he was using a regular camera, not a digital type, with a large magnifying lens like you would see on a professional photographer's camera. With no way to view what he had on the camera, we gave him the option of throwing the camera off the pier into the ocean or being detained by us. He promptly chose option one and threw the very expensive camera off the pier and into the gulf.

When our search pits got real busy, we QRF would be called to their location to assist in overwatch of people and to help search vehicles. These were almost always large white truck convoys, normally fifty or more trucks that we would be called to assist with. The drivers of these trucks were all TCNs (third country nationals). There wasn't much of a vetting process done on these guys, so you had to spend the time and do a very thorough search on all their trucks. They were not allowed to have weapons of any sort, cameras, drugs, alcohol, or maps of the inside of our bases. There are a couple of incidents worth mentioning that I ran into while assisting with these searches.

My QRF truck was requested to assist with searching a large white truck convoy. When we got there, two of the guys from my gun truck and I went into the search pit and began helping the other three soldiers from my unit with the daunting task of searching probably seventy-five semi-trucks and trailers. On probably the third truck I searched, I saw a spiral notebook and pen lying on the console. You didn't see many of these as most of these guys were illiterate. So I grabbed it and flipped a few pages. I noticed crude drawings of what appeared to be ECPs, and most of the writing was in Arabic, so I didn't understand what in the hell it said. However, toward the back of the notebook, there was some writing in English, specifically "Kill Americans." I could make out *soldiers* written a few times as well. I took this over to our interpreter and also found out who the driver in the search pit holding area was. We placed him in flex cuffs and, with the interpreter's help, asked him about the notebook. He wasn't giving up anything, so my higher called KCID in to deal with him.

The same two guys rolled up in a white Suburban, both dressed in bright-white man dresses and aviators just like the last time. Again, it was a completely ridiculous sight; and again, they had guns and other gear, but they were all just thrown about in their Suburban. They spoke with us briefly and took the statements that we had prepared for them and all the evidence to include the notebook we had collected. After putting it in their Suburban, the skinny dude in his white man dress and aviators walked over to the TCN, got within six inches of his face, and said a couple of words to him in Arabic. The TCN just stared at the ground at this point and didn't say a word. The sand on the ground around the TCN, I noticed, was turning dark. It took me a second to realize what had just happened. He was pissing himself out of fear. I was watching it roll off his dirt-stained feet and sandals onto the ground. Still to this day, I have no idea what the KCID guys would tell these guys in Arabic, but whatever it was sure struck fear into them. They took him away like they had done the time before, and we never saw him again. I asked our local interpreter again what was going to be his fate. He simply said they have a zero-tolerance policy. I took that to mean he would probably be executed.

Probably my most stressful call of the deployment happened at this same search pit on a white truck convoy. My QRF truck was called to help search a large seventy-five-plus truck convoy. When these convoys lined up in the search pit, they knew that they were to open all compartments of the vehicle and they were to shut the engines and all electronics off. This also meant to open all doors on the trucks and trailers and also the hood, glove box, console, etc. After doing this, the drivers exited the search pit and signed in and went to the holding area until our search was completed.

Well, when we started searching, we noticed one of the semis' engine was still running and the hood was shut. As I approached it, I could see an odd-shaped canister through the grill of the truck with what looked to be possible wires running into it. I just backed away from it after writing down the plate numbers so I could identify the driver. We were able to get the driver out of the holding area, and he couldn't speak any English of course. He looked Middle Eastern. I can't remember where he was from though. Our interpreter was a Kuwaiti civilian at the search pit, and he was not about to reenter the search pit with me as it was not in the contract he had with us. So I grabbed the TCN by the collar on the back of his shirt and pushed him into the search pit. He was reluctant and didn't want to walk where I was pushing him. This was another red flag to me. At this point, I drew my Beretta M9 pistol from my holster and buried the muzzle of it to the back of his head. This cleared things up a bit, and he quickly learned how to walk again.

We made the one-hundred-yard walk with my right hand grasping a handful of his shirt collar and my left hand grasping my pistol, finger firmly on the trigger with the muzzle pressed against his head. My heart was racing as we approached the still-running truck. In English, I told him to raise the hood of the truck. I reached around the side of him, kicking the hood with my right foot as I said it since I didn't have a free hand. He muttered some stuff in Arabic that I didn't understand. At this point, I pushed him to the cab of the truck, where he pulled the hood release. Then we went back around to the front, and he opened it. This whole time I was just waiting to be blown up. I figured, well, at least he will be in front of me if we do. Now with the hood open and truck still running, I could see the suspected IED very clearly. It looked like an intact two-liter Mountain Dew bottle lined with tin foil inside. It had a hose going into it and a red and black wire taped to the back of it with black electrical tape that wrapped around the bottle in two places. I could not see where the wires went to, and I also could not see where the hose went to. I left the truck running and cautiously walked backward out of the search pit, dragging the TCN by the collar with my pistol still pressed to the back of his head. Once we made it out of the search pit and behind the blast walls, we flex-cuffed the TCN and called in Army EOD. I gave them a detailed description of what I had found. A few hours later, EOD was on site, and they were able to clear it. They said it was more than likely a probe to see if we would find it. If not, we would have gotten a real one the next time. The TCN was turned over to KCID, and like the others, we never saw him again.

In that same search pit, I had one of the weirdest calls I had ever gotten as well. My QRF truck was called to the search pit without much of a situation report over the radio, which was odd. When we got there, I was met by the search pit's NCOIC, and he asked me to come with him into the pit. As we were walking there, he prepared me for the gory mess I was about to see. He said there was blood everywhere and all kinds of large chunks of meat hanging from the ceilings of all these semis. No one in the search area had ever seen anything like it.

I looked at the first three trucks, and they were all the same: they had parachute cord, otherwise known as 550 cord, ran across the ceilings of their trucks with thin-sliced chucks of fresh meat hanging. This was a rather gross sight, as blood was still dripping from the meat as we were looking at it. While the TCNs were driving, the meat must have been swinging back and forth. This caused blood to drip everywhere inside the cab of their trucks to include the inside of the windshields and all over the dash. I looked at the other NCO and told him they were making jerky out of whatever this was. Being from rural Ohio, I was an avid deer hunter and had made my fair share of jerky. These TCN truck drivers just improvised and had hung it in the cabs of their trucks to dry in the 120°F heat. We went back and got our interpreter and asked one of the drivers what it was and why it was hanging from the ceilings of their trucks. He said it was a camel that had been hit in the road in front of their convoy. They stopped and collectively butchered it and sliced it into crude strips for jerky. He offered us some, which we tactfully declined.

Another strange call we got was from a navy tower on the end of one of our piers at the SPOD. They reported floating human body parts in the water off the end of the pier. We rushed to their location. When we got there, it was a severed human foot washed up against the pier. We called KCID too, as this was more their lane and it really didn't have anything to do with us. When they arrived, they walked over, looked at it, and said, "Yep, that is a foot." They were not the least bit concerned about it. They told us to give them a call if we get a whole body. They said that happens a lot and to just leave it alone, so we did. Everyone just drove off and went back to what they were doing. I have never found a severed foot here in America, but I would like to think local authorities would at least scoop it out of the water, bag it, and take a report or something. That just shows you how different the cultures around the world are.

By far, the best night I had while on QRF was when we got a call about someone taking suspected pictures of one of our ships off the end of one of the piers. Our truck responded, and we found three guys fishing off the end of the pier. I got out and made contact with them; two were Filipino, and one guy was an American civilian from Hawaii. I checked the camera and deleted a few of the pictures with questionable backgrounds. We had about six hours of our shift left, so we decided to hang out with these guys and fish a little with them. It was a blast. I caught my first eel and shark that night. The shark was a blacktip and probably just over two feet long. They were catching ocean catfish and sharks for a fish fry they were going to have. Not long after that night, our unit would head back to Fort Hood, Texas, to demobilize and then fly back to Ohio and reintegrate back to our civilian lives.

Fishing off the pier at the SPOD

Me with a black tip shark

Sun Rise at the SPOD
Photo credit of SGT Tyler Wallace

SGT Zac Allen, Iraq

July 2009–June 2010

In the beginning of June 2009, Zac was a week out from leaving for his AT (annual training) with the Ohio Army National Guard when he received a warning order from the Army National Guard. He would not be attending AT with his parent unit, the 211th Maintenance Company, like he thought; he would instead be going with the 1483rd Transportation Company. He would be what was known as a cross-level in the army. That is what a soldier is referred to when they are pulled out of their organic unit and attached to a different unit of assignment to fill a slot that was short for a deployment. This had become a common occurrence as the war on terror dragged on and on. The warning order stated that the 1483rd TC would be called to active duty in 2009 to deploy in support of Operation Iraqi Freedom. Zac's rank at the time was specialist (SPC) E-4 with an MOS of generator repairer.

A week later at AT, he was told he was going to be a gunner in one of the trucks that would be providing security for the convoys. He started training to do that in preparation for the upcoming deployment. It didn't take long, though, for Zac's maintenance warrant officer to realize he would be better utilized in the maintenance section of the unit, as Zac was an energetic, hardworking soldier capable of more than just working on generators or being a gunner on convoys. From the end of that first AT with the 1483rd, he would be one of the main mechanics of the unit, working on everything from their prime movers, which were HETS (Heavy Equipment Transport System), to generators, and anything in between.

Sometime between that AT and the time he left for his mobilization site, Zac was over at his longtime neighbor Bill Maple's house. He had stopped to talk to Bill and tell him about his upcoming deployment, as he had always looked up to Bill since he had also worn the uniform and was a Vietnam veteran. While Zac was there, Bill's brother Jesse stopped by upon hearing the news. Jesse drove the short couple-mile drive home, grabbed the Bible that so many had carried into harm's way before, and gave it to Zac. When Jesse Maple gave the Bible to Zac at Bill's house that day, he told Zac about everyone who had carried it before and how they had come back alive. He also told him to keep his head down and good luck.

About a week before deployment, Zac received a phone call from his brother-in-law Zac Miller, who asked him to stop by his house. When Zac got there, he was handed Miller's Bible that he had carried in his 2004–2005 deployment to Iraq and again in his 2008 deployment to Kuwait. This Bible was in a plastic bag that he had used to protect it from the weather and from sweat that would have ruined it otherwise. It just so happened to be the same sturdy plastic bag that the Bible had been placed into in 2004 when Miller had carried it and Jesse's Bible both in it. The bag actually had come out of an MRE (Meal, Ready to Eat). It was a heavy-duty bag made to mix a drink powder packet and water in. Miller didn't know that Zac already was given Jesse's Bible and that Zac would end up putting them both in that same bag for the duration of his deployment to Iraq. I actually didn't figure this out until 2019 when I was writing this book. Miller told Zac to carry it and that it was lucky and it would bring him the same luck.

Zac would go to Camp Atterbury, Indiana, to do his mobilization training, and on September 11, 2009, his unit would head to Indianapolis Airport to fly out for Kuwait. He still recalls that day. He is not a really superstitious person, but that day was full of bad omens. First, it was September 11. Any soldier of today's generation is probably a little uneasy about getting on a jet on September 11, but there was another weird thing when they were boarding the jet with another unit. Zac asked them what patch they were wearing, and they said 3 triple 6, or 3666. Zac thought in his head, *Really, I am flying into a combat zone on September 11 with a unit I don't know named 666? Wow, here is your sign.*

The flight turned out to be uneventful as it went from Indianapolis, Indiana, to Germany and then onto Kuwait. After the 1483rd got to Kuwait, they would go through a few more weeks' worth of training and equipment issue at Camp Buehring before heading north to Iraq. The unit would fly on a C-17 from Kuwait to Balad Air Base, where the majority of the unit, being 88M truck drivers, would double up with a HET company whose convoy was headed to Taji. Zac, being in maintenance, kind of lucked out and was able to take a Black Hawk helicopter from Balad to Taji.

Once in Taji, Zac would be working out of a maintenance shop his platoon took over. Zac's first priority would be light sets that were all around post. These light sets were vital to the entire post, as many people relied on them to run twenty-four-hour operations. His second priority was the HETs; these were the prime movers his unit was there to operate. These trucks were responsible for moving all the heavy armor and other heavy loads all over the theater. From Abrams battle tanks to construction equipment, they hauled it all. Zac's third priority was generators' maintenance and repair. He excelled at his job, and during this deployment, he was promoted to sergeant and eventually became nightshift NCOIC, which means he was in charge of all maintenance operations during that shift.

A volunteer mission came down from the higher-ups to field two MSTs (maintenance support teams) to go to a remote FOB and provide maintenance assets to 1483's convoys on the other side of Iraq on the Iranian border. Zac jumped at the opportunity and volunteered for the mission. He was then sent to a tiny FOB (forward operating base) named Camp Caldwell. This was a small FOB on the northeastern border of Iran. The MSTs loaded up all their equipment onto their trucks and convoyed across Iraq from Taji to Camp Caldwell. The MSTs would set up and work out of Caldwell for a little over three weeks. Zac said the air was red almost the entire time they were there. Red air translates into very limited ground movement, as your air support was not cleared to fly normally; this is due to air quality. Limited movement of convoys meant the MSTs had little to no work. The decision was made by the higher-ups to bring them back to Taji, where maintenance was still in high demand. There was a high enemy threat at the time of the Camp Caldwell mission; however, Zac said it was rather quiet. A few occasional bursts of small arms fire and the rare single-mortar round here and there.

Zac did have a few close calls while on Taji. On one of the major Islamic holidays, a few insurgents breached the wire and killed a few of the contracted security guards who were on the post. Zac said he heard this happen as he was walking back to his living area from his night shift duties in the motor pool. He said it was a little over a quarter mile away from him; he heard an explosion and a bunch of small arms fire. He didn't know at the time what had happened; he had no idea that they made it through the wire. He said he saw the base QRFs (US Army soldiers) respond to the scene, and they killed the insurgents. Until that point, Zac just figured it was some sort of celebratory gunfire as that was commonplace around Islamic holidays and special events.

Zac said he also had a few close calls with mortar rounds; he said Taji at that time would probably get one or two rounds in a week. Usually, he said, an Apache would respond to them and quickly dispatch any threat. After this, everything would quiet down for a week or so, then it would happen again. One night, Zac was walking from his maintenance bays to his battalion headquarters when a mortar round landed directly on the other side of a double-walled HESCO barrier from him. He said the concussion from the blast knocked him to the ground, his ears instantly ringing. It was just one single round; it was the closest Zac had ever been to an incoming mortar round. A HESCO barrier is a wire mesh container that has a heavy-duty fabric liner; they measure roughly four feet by four feet. The military uses these filled with sand and dirt for blast protection.

A little while later in the deployment, he would have another close call. Late in the deployment, the maintenance guys were getting hammered on by higher-ups to wear all their safety PPE (personal protective equipment) and to put a higher standard on safety. Of course, Zac, being a joker, decided to step it up a notch. He decided to don all his PPE that he had in the bay. He was wearing a hard hat, earplugs, ear muffs, safety glasses, face shield, gloves, and a few other things. After donning all this, he proceeded to straddle an engine that they just put on the crude engine test dyno they had. He was in the process of test running it wide-open when a huge, ground-shaking *boom* was heard. His heart stopped for a split second; he thought that the engine he was straddling had exploded between his legs. After he realized he wasn't hurt and that the engine hadn't exploded, he took off the muffs and earplugs. That was when he realized a mortar round landed right outside their maintenance bay.

Shortly after that incident, Zac and the 1483rd TC would leave Iraq for Kuwait and then onto Camp Atterbury, Indiana for demobilization.

CW2 Zac Miller, Kuwait, Iraq, and Syria

April 2017–April 2018

In November 2016, word came down again that my unit would be deploying to the Middle East, this time in support of Operation Enduring Freedom. We would mobilize in the spring of 2017 out of Springfield, Ohio, and head to Fort Hood, Texas, to do our mobilization training before leaving for Kuwait. My unit was the 371st Sustainment Brigade out of Springfield, Ohio. Our mission would be to oversee and manage all sustainment assets in OIR (Operation Inherent Resolve). This was the fight against ISIS in Iraq and Syria. Also, OSS (Operation Spartan Shield) was the mission in the Middle East meant to deter Iranian aggression. This meant we would have personnel all over the Middle East in places like Kuwait, Jordan, Iraq, Syria, Qatar, and even a few in Afghanistan.

As a sustainment brigade, we pretty much tracked and ran everything in the entire battlefield. The only thing we didn't touch was combat operational planning. We were in charge of all the logistics of the war. My small piece of the pie was supposed to be all armament maintenance for the theater, which meant I was responsible for everything that shoots, basically, ground wise—no aviation assets. So I would review all maintenance reports from throughout the theater for trends or problem issues that were popping up, anything from an M9 pistol a soldier would be carrying on their hip to an M1 Abrams main battle tank.

That is what an armament warrant officer at a sustainment brigade is supposed to be doing. However, in the modern army, we do more with less, so my heavy maintenance section—made up of a captain, three chief warrant officers, and an additional eleven NCOs—was stripped down to myself, Master Sergeant Derringer, Staff Sergeant McMurray, and Sergeant Harris. I was acting as four roles: OIC (officer in charge), automotive, armament, and electronics warrants for the section; Master Sergeant Derringer was acting as NCOIC of our stripped-down section; while Staff Sergeant McMurray, and Sergeant Harris were doing the work in the trenches, so to speak. Their jobs would be compiling all reports and data from all the down-trace units in theater, turning it into readable documents for me, and putting key information on slide decks so I would be able to brief it to my colonels and generals whenever asked about any maintenance issues in theater, which was almost daily to one of them. We were a busy section at times, as you could imagine, as were most sections in my unit during the deployment.

This was a huge adjustment for me as I was used to being the warfighter at the other end of this massive chain of army logistics. But what my last two deployments had taught me was how it sucked to be that warfighter who was in need of something to do his or her job and didn't have the assets they needed to do it, whether it is that mechanic who didn't have the right part or tool to complete the job or that infantryman or artilleryman who needed ammunition to continue the fight. That was what our unit was there to provide. My job over there was pretty lackluster until August 2017 when one of the Eighty-Second Airborne's M777 artillery pieces had a catastrophic accident when firing on ISIS in Mosul, Iraq. This accident left two of their paratroopers dead and injured five others. SGT Roshain Brooks and SGT Allen Stigler Jr. were the two paratroopers killed by this mishap.

I got a call the next day wanting me to do an investigation as to why this happened. I would be part of a team that would do the investigation; as an armament chief, my job would be the mechanical part of the investigation, scrubbing maintenance records and actually looking at the artillery piece and trying to figure out what had happened that night. I am not able to disclose the findings of this investigation, but there were multiple factors that led to the deadly mishap. Within a week, I would say, of this happening, I received another call that another issue happened with an M777 155mm howitzer, this time in Raqqa, Syria. A round had cooked off in a howitzer as the breech was closing; luckily, by some miracle, none of the crew was injured. I would be going there to be part of that investigation as well. Armament was all of a sudden a top priority in the theater.

I flew out of Erbil, Iraq, on an Osprey under the cover of darkness for a remote, undisclosed location near the city of Raqqa, Syria. We landed using a vertical landing there, and the four of us exited the Osprey while it was still running under the cover of darkness. Once we were clear of the aircraft, it took off with another vertical takeoff prop, washing us with sand and all kinds of other debris. After it flew off and you could hear again, I heard a voice out of the darkness. It was one of the marine infantrymen that were sent out to meet us and escort us to the gunline. I say gunline, as this was not a FOB like I was used to. This was the textbook definition of an austere location. There was no concertina wire around the perimeter of the gunline; they just had the M777A2s pointing forward with an artilleryman manning crew-served weapons as well on the front, and a few sections of marine infantrymen pushed out a little and set up fighting positions around the rear for rear security. Since I was in a brigade staff position with no need for them, I didn't have any NVGs (night vision goggles) on me, so I had no choice but to ruck toward the gunline under the cover of complete darkness. The three gentlemen with me in my inspection team didn't have NVGs either. I was just focused on the marine radioman (RTO) in front of me.

We were walking in a column since the area hadn't been completely cleared of possible mines or IEDs. I was the third one from the front: the SSG squad leader, followed by the RTO, and I was next. I had three other members of the inspection team behind me. They were all loaded down with heavy rucks and other equipment just like I was. Then I believe three other marines followed up on rear security. We walked for a couple hundred yards when I saw the RTO's silhouette in front of me gradually go down what appeared to be a slight decline. He was about 5 meters in front of me. A few steps later, when I went to put my foot down, there was no ground. It was a horrible feeling, but it was too late—I was already committed. I fell three feet, I would estimate, and just completely ate shit. Luckily, I landed on my knees for the most part. I was able to keep ahold of my M4 as well; however, the 100 lbs of gear I was carrying on me at the time basically drove me into the ground hard. I ended up hitting my chin on the buttstock of my own rifle and cutting it pretty bad and messing up my neck pretty good. With that added weight from my gear, ruck, and other stuff, it jacked me up.

It happened very quickly. I was able to get up on my own quickly thanks to adrenaline. The marine SSG was standing in front of me, apologizing he had forgotten we were not wearing NVGs. I remember telling him not to worry about it, I was good. I asked him what the hell it was that I had fell into. He said it was a VBIED (vehicle-born improvised explosive device) ditch that they had hired a local guy with a track hoe to dig for them as part of their security measures. We had started walking again at this point, and as the SSG was turned around talking quietly to me while walking backward, his silhouette disappeared from my vision as he fell and ate shit in a second VBIED ditch. I remember thinking at this point, "What the hell have I gotten myself into, and why in the hell did I not bring my NVGs?" He got up and brushed himself off. He assured us that was the last ditch we would have to cross that night.

The marines had a gradual slope they had dug out that was about a foot wide, if that, and that went down into those ditches and back up the other side. This way, on their foot patrols, they could walk right across those ditches. The ditches were there to stop suicide-bombing terrorist from driving a vehicle at a high rate of speed toward their position and blowing them up, which was one of the most effective tools the enemy had at killing American troops in the Middle East.

Once we were on the gunline, I noticed how much of an austere environment we were actually in. They had one small tent for their TOC (tactical operations center). These marines were sleeping in holes they had dug with absolutely no creature comforts. By creature comforts, I mean running water, hot chow, tents to sleep in, AC, or even an outhouse. They were literally shitting in bags. Grunts in the field refer to these as WAG bags. I believe these are a rather new invention probably since the soldiers from the early years of the Iraq and Afghanistan wars were having health problems and concerns from the burn pits. The military was getting away from burning all their waste materials as much as possible to include human waste. This was my first exposure to WAG bags, and it was a little weird at first. But like everything else, you adapt and get used to it. I got there in the beginning of September, and these guys had been out here since May. Their uniforms were falling apart, holes through all their pants and shirts. A few of them had the soles of their combat boots taped on with 100-mile-an-hour tape, the military's version of duct tape. I asked a few of these marines why they couldn't get gear replaced. Boiled down, they just didn't have supply lines like the army does. Also, they had come off a MEU (marine expeditionary unit), so that means they came off a ship and didn't expect to be out in Syria for six months. I think they told me they expected only a month or two, so they packed a light bag with two uniforms and all their combat gear.

These marines were firing into the city of Raqqa. This was ISIS's (Daesh) self-proclaimed capital city of their caliphate, which spanned two countries, at that time Syria and Iraq. I arrived the beginning of September, and these marines had already fired thirty-six thousand rounds of 155mm out of five guns. They did this into this city that once had a civilian population of one million people before Daesh took over. In 2015, while under Daesh control, it was estimated at four hundred thousand. In 2018, after being liberated from Daesh, it was estimated to have a population of one hundred sixty-five thousand. Over 80 percent of Raqqa was left uninhabitable as a result of this battle.

As I stated, these marines had fired thirty-six thousand rounds of artillery, which is a staggering amount, almost completely unheard of in today's militaries. These devil dogs were loving it; they were finally getting to do what they had trained to, and they were inflicting severe casualties on Daesh. If the SDF (Syrian Democratic Forces) made up of mostly Kurds ran into any issues, such as snipers or any stiff resistance of any sort, they would fall back to cover, and the US advisor that was imbedded with them, I was told an Army Ranger, would call for fire. That is when these devil dogs would jump into action, going from zero to sixty in just seconds, putting whatever type of rounds were called for on target.

This was some of the most rewarding time I had spent in the military. I met and got to know all these guys while working on their guns with them. Two of the gun chiefs were actually from Ohio as well. One was from Troy, Ohio, Sergeant Christman, and another Staff Sergeant was from the Cleveland area. Sergeant Christman and I hit it off, and I spent any downtime I had at his gun. Gun 1 for the most part, talking about fishing, hunting, and vehicles, as he was into that stuff like I was. He also had a radio that he only allowed country music to be played on, which I obviously liked. I would rotate in on the guns and was able to fire quite a few missions with them. I really enjoyed this. How many armament warrants ever get a chance to put live rounds on the enemy? I would venture to say less than 1 percent of them. Usually, we are stuck working on them and figuring out the hard issues, whether it be mechanical or simply getting the right equipment or parts for the job. These guys didn't just let me fire once; they basically threw me the keys to the car. They said, "Chief, you can fire as much as you want." I fired my first mission from gun two; it was four rounds of HE (high explosive) on September 9, 2017. I still have the spent primer from that first round fired on enemy in combat on my shelf at home as a war trophy.

SGT Christman gun one's gun chief
Photo credit of Matt Callahan

But by far the most rewarding feeling I had was on September 11, 2017: a call for fire can down for an Excalibur round to be fired. Sergeant Christman had promised me the honors of firing it if we ever got the call for one when I was near his gun. An Excalibur round is a GPS-guided round that actually has a rocket motor on the back of it for extended range, allowing it to reach out to more than 50 kilometers and is accurate within 2 meters. These rounds are so rare that only 1,400 have ever been fired in combat as of August 14, 2019. These marines had almost all fired one as well. I was told the one I fired hit an ISIS sniper that had an SDF pinned down. I still cannot think of a better thing to do as an American on September 11. This single shot made my entire career in the military worth it. I personally felt a slight bit of justice was served with that round.

One other thing happened that day that I will never forget. It was around noon. All four of the guns on the line were attached an American flag to three sections of camo net pole and were raised in an act of defiance to ISIS, or patriotism, as you will. They only left them up for maybe a half hour. But for that half hour, you felt damn proud to be an American at the tip of the spear raining steel death on these ISIS scumbags.

M777 Howitzer silhouetted as sunsets on Raqqa, Syria

Mechanically, their guns were in rough shape, as they had very limited maintenance support. One corporal to be exact with a small hand carried a tool kit and no repair parts. They had already set one gun off-line by the time I had gotten there because it was the one that had the round cooked off in it, the whole reason I was there. It also had some other issues. I pullover-gauged it and determined the gun tube was shot out of it so that gun became the parts gun. The other four howitzers were able to continue their uninterrupted twenty-four-hour all-weather fires support operations because of this parts gun. They would end up wearing the gun tubes out on three of the five howitzers they were assigned, which can be directly contributed to how much firing they were doing. By the time I had left, I had written up a report that allowed them to get four new howitzers sent to their location. My team also was able to conclude the reason that they had a round cook off in the gun tube. By watching and observing the crews during their firing, it was determined that when the one cannon crew member would swab the chamber with a wet swab between shots at night, he had run out of water in the can he would put his swab into and thus was swabbing the chamber with a dry swab and not realizing it at the time. That shows just how heavy the volume of fire was at times. We briefed findings to all crew members and their leadership so they could implement extra crew safety checks to ensure this would not be a future issue that could result in the deaths of the crew members and unnecessary damage to the howitzer as well. In our brief, we also included safety checks we had learned from investigating the Eighty-Second Airborne's M777 just a few weeks earlier.

I left the gunline in Raqqa and headed to TLB, a very small FOB in Syria, and briefed the marine LTC (lieutenant colonel) who was in charge there on the situation of the howitzers. Then after a couple days, we flew out under the cover of darkness again on an Osprey headed for Erbil, Iraq, and then, after a short stay, headed back to Kuwait. I ended up staying in Kuwait for the rest of my time on this deployment, monitoring the fall of ISIS from briefings and slideshows at the brigade staff level while spending my time briefing the colonels and generals on their maintenance assets in theater. I ended up leaving Kuwait in March 2018 to fly back to Fort Hood, Texas, so our unit could demobilize. This took about a week, and then we flew back home to Ohio for our welcome home ceremony in Springfield, Ohio. This was one of the happiest days of my life, being reunited with my wife and our two kids. The last two deployments I had done were both longer, but I didn't have a family in the first one. Breann and I were still dating at the time. The second one we had gotten married before, so I would have to leave a wife at home. Those were both hard, but leaving two small children for a year to go off to war tears you up inside. I was awarded a Meritorious Service Medal (MSM) and a Combat Action Badge (CAB) from this deployment. I would end up getting promoted to Chief Warrant Officer 3 (CW3) upon returning to home station in Ohio.

COL Betts pinning my Combat Action Badge on at Ft Hood, TX

SGT Will Allen, Afghanistan
March 20, 2018–March 20, 2019

In 2018, Will had been in the Ohio Army National Guard for ten years as a 91F small arms / artillery repairer. He had made the rank of sergeant and was holding an staff sergeant slot. He just needed to complete his NCOES school so he could be promoted. He was wanting to deploy so he could earn that coveted veteran status a reserve soldier or national guardsman gets after getting deployed. He had turned in 160 forms in the past, which is the form that the National Guard needs to add you to the list of volunteers to pull from. If you are on this list, you are volunteering to deploy with any unit in the state. So after a couple of years of getting nowhere with the guard, Will started looking into other options. One of these was civilian contracting. He ended up signing a one-year contract with AC First to be an artillery inspector / repairer in Afghanistan. Will was so passionate about this he resigned the full-time job he had with the Ohio Army National Guard, who was not supportive of this decision to pursue this one-year contract in Afghanistan. There were perks to this—well, actually just one—great pay. Will was planning on building a home on some property he owned, and a deployment would have really helped this. But by being a civilian contractor, he was able to more than triple what he would have made on that one-year deployment with the army.

Before Will shipped out, he was called up by Jesse Maple, who asked him to come to his house. When Will arrived like so many guys before, Jesse and his wife Cheryl greeted him and invited him into their home. Jesse had known Will since he was a baby but never really talked to him one-on-one about his time in the service or his Bible. Jesse was brief but explained to Will what the little pocket Bible meant to him and how it was able to bring everyone who had carried it in the past back from war alive. Will took the Bible that day from Jesse and carried it with him from Ohio to the United Arab Emirates and then onto Afghanistan.

He was one of six inspectors in Afghanistan supporting the army's artillery, which was M777s (155mm) and M119s (105mm) howitzers. These inspectors were spread all over the country at six different FOBs during his time in Afghanistan: KAF (Kandahar), BAF (Bagram), JBAD (Fenty), Gamberi, Dalhke, and Dwyer. Will ended up in charge of the guns on Fenty and Gamberi, although he traveled to a few of the other locations during his year in Afghanistan.

The units Will was supporting were the Fourth ID, Third ID, and toward the end of his year, the 118th FA Georgia Army National Guard as they came in and replaced the Third and Fourth IDs' active duty soldiers. While supporting these guns, Will lived just like the army Joes—he slept in a tent or a small wooded building, depending on what FOB he was on. His quarters were always within 150 yards of the gunline. Out at the remote FOBs, contractors didn't get all the creature comforts that they did living in Kuwait or even at the larger FOBs like KAF or BAF in Afghanistan. He spent his days hanging out on the gunline with the gun crews, working on whatever needed repaired or serviced. Any downtime he had was spent watching the gun crews conduct fire missions or just hanging out with them talking, as there was not a whole lot else to do.

Will said that while he was at Fenty, they never took any incoming rounds at all. But while he was living in Gamberi, they had incoming mortar rounds a few times. One of the times was a little too close for Will's comfort. He said he could hear the whistle from them. They hit a building not far from where Will was standing, but no one was seriously injured. A few soldiers had very minor wounds was all. Outside the FOB, Will said a few of the convoys were hit, and on one instance, a few fuel trucks were blown up. This happened very close to post, the black smoke from the burning trucks completely engulfed the FOB for a while until the tanker finished burning. Will would remain at Gamberi until he came home in March 2019. Upon returning home, Will went out to Jesse's house and promptly returned the Bible that he had kept with him in his pack for the entire year.

Sergeant Allen is still serving in the Ohio Army National Guard as a small arms / artillery repairer. He is still waiting on that call to go to war as a soldier so he can use the skills he honed and perfected as a civilian contractor on the battlefield of Afghanistan.

Both bibles mine and Jesse's

In Conclusion

These two Bibles have been to hell on earth and back ten times now, and the soldiers carrying them have all made it back alive. These Bibles gave the soldiers carrying them comfort, knowing that they had something with them they could turn to in dark times if they needed something to boost their faith in God or just wanted to read in times of need. Some carried it more as a good luck charm and never cracked the cover of it. But one thing all these soldiers had in common was that they knew that their God was with them watching over them and giving them the courage to continue the mission at hand.

The soldiers who have carried these two bibles have amassed quite a few awards. Some of the more prominent awards they have received are three bronze stars with "V" device for valor, one Meritorious Service Medal, a Vietnam Cross of Gallantry, two Purple Hearts, two Combat Infantryman Badges (CIB), and a Combat Action Badge (CAB).

About the Author

Zac Miller was born in 1983 and grew up in the small town of West Lafayette, Ohio. He knew at a young age that he wanted to serve his county. He spent all his free time as a child playing army with his neighborhood friends. He came from a long family of veterans; both of Zac's grandfathers served. One was a WWII veteran, and the other served during the Korean War. His father served in the Air Force during the Vietnam War and in the Army National Guard during Desert Storm. In his teenage years, Zac knew he wanted to serve and jumped at the first opportunity he was presented with. At the age of seventeen and a junior in high school, he joined the Army National Guard with his parents' consent.

He was working on a local farm at the time with a friend named Jared Lillo. They spent countless hours together picking sweet corn and pumpkins, baling hay, and doing whatever else needed to be done. During this time, they decided to join on the buddy plan, which allowed them to pick their job in the military and would ensure that they went to the same unit of assignment. Talking to the recruiter, Zac wanted to become an armament repairman, which is a military term for a gunsmith. Jared wanted to become a wheeled vehicle mechanic. The recruiter explained to them that they would try to get them these jobs but made them pick a secondary job just in case he couldn't get two slots in the same unit. So they both picked 11B Infantry as a secondary choice. It appeared that they were going to have to go for infantry because of manning issues. So for that reason, they were sent to Fort Benning, Georgia, home of the infantry, for their basic training, which they attended between their junior and senior years in high school. Unlike most horror stories you hear about military recruiters not taking care of their recruits, Zac's did; and when the time came, he was actually able to get them both into their first choice of jobs since they had not done AIT (advanced individual training) yet. They would end up at the 211th Maintenance Company in Newark, Ohio, for their first duty station.

Zac graduated high school in 2002 and tried his hand at college, attending Hocking College with intentions of becoming a game warden. He didn't enjoy college that much, and when the opportunity came, he was hired full-time by the Ohio Army National Guard to work as a small arms repairman. Zac ended up working full-time for the Guard until November 2016 when we has hired as a county veteran service officer for Coshocton County.

Zac's military experience includes three deployments to the Middle East, the first one in 2004 and the last one being in 2017-18. He started his career enlisted as a private and worked his way to sergeant. After ten years in the service, he was ready for a change and put his packet in to become a warrant officer. His packet went through, and he went to Warrant Officer Candidate School and was promoted to the rank of warrant officer 1 in 2011. He is still serving our great nation as a chief warrant officer 3 and has twenty years and counting of service at the time this book was being published.

While Chief Miller is still serving, he has a double life as a civilian. He married his high school sweetheart, Breann, in 2007, and they have two children together. He started a small business in 2011, Black Rifle Customs LLC, where he sells new and used firearms and does gunsmithing. He is also the director / county veteran service officer for Coshocton County's Veterans Service Office, where he enjoys his other passion: taking care of fellow veterans and their families by helping them get the benefits they have earned.

He volunteers his time serving his fellow veterans as a director on the board of a local nonprofit, Operation Veterans Helping Veterans (OVHV). He is also a member of the Coshocton County Honor Guard, which performs military honors at veterans' funerals around the county. At these military funerals, he can normally be found acting in the commander's role, folding the flag and presenting it to the next of kin of the deceased veteran.

CPSIA information can be obtained
at www.ICGtesting.com
Printed in the USA
BVHW031131270420
578609BV00001B/46